CREATIVE INTELLIGENCE

CQ@Play

ENDORSEMENTS

Cherylene de Jager and Anton Muller have written a helpful book for those interested in the many angles and theories bouncing around the big idea of creativity. It's all the more welcome as they are South African academics and practitioners, building local capability and insight into an area that is of critical Importance in growing, diversifying and transitioning a South African economy that has changed little in its basic construction over the last 20 years. It's high time we brought more creative acumen to business and government and more business acumen to creatives – and government. This book is an encouraging step on the way.

Jon Foster-Pedley, Dean and director, Henley Business School, Africa

This work combines sound academic research and carefully selected tools to develop Creative Intelligence (CQ) for the 'I'm not creative' business leader, professional and anyone else who has the courage to develop their CQ. Creativity is not magic, it's a skill that can be developed. CQ@Play cleverly showcases the essence of creativity, innovation and design thinking in solving real, local problems.

Michael Jordaan, founder and CEO of Montegray Capital

The nature of work is changing. Is your organisation prepared to keep up? In this book, De Jager and Muller have put together a roadmap to navigate changes on the horizon and a toolkit of resources to grow and nurture the creativity you'll need to make the journey. This is the field guide in your expedition to new levels of innovation.

David Burkus, author of UNDER NEW MANAGEMENT and MYTHS OF CREATIVITY

A must read for anyone interested in unlocking their potential for the 4IR. A practical guide on How, When, What and Which methodologies, frameworks, techniques and tools to use. Organisations and individuals seeking to convert creative potential into commercial application, will find the How to achieve it. Creative intelligence is a long-term investment that needs commitment and endurance. – this book makes the journey enjoyable.

Coenie Middel CA(SA) Chairman: Middel & Partners

Read this practical book on Creative Intelligence and up both your game, and the performance of your business.

Cherylene has many years at the sharp end of helping organisations to profit from releasing the potential of employee creativity across the whole organisation.

Dr Nick Marsh, Consultant in Strategic Foresight, author of ALL STAR COMPANY, and STRATEGIC FORESIGHT: THE POWER OF STANDING IN THE FUTURE, The Next Corporation, Cambridge, New Zealand.

An amazing must-read bursting with big ideas that focus on creativity and the tools with which to encourage and develop it in your organisation. This is a practical book that will change how you think and transform your individual and organisational creative competitiveness. The South African focus is an ode to local Creative Intelligence in action.

Sharmla Chetty, President – Global Markets Africa, Asia, Europe, USA, Duke Corporate Education

Copyright © KR Publishing and Dr Cherylene De Jager

All reasonable steps have been taken to ensure that the contents of this book do not, directly or indirectly, infringe any existing copyright of any third person and, further, that all quotations or extracts taken from any other publication or work have been appropriately acknowledged and referenced. The publisher, editors and printers take no responsibility for any copyright infringement committed by an author of this work.

Copyright subsists in this work. No part of this work may be reproduced in any form or by any means without the written consent of the publisher or the author.

While the publisher, editors and printers have taken all reasonable steps to ensure the accuracy of the contents of this work, they take no responsibility for any loss or damage suffered by any person as a result of that person relying on the information contained in this work.

First published in 2020.

ISBN: 978-1-86922-830-9
eISBN: 978-1-86922-831-6

Published by KR Publishing
P O Box 3954
Randburg
2125
Republic of South Africa

Tel: (011) 706-6009
Fax: (011) 706-1127
E-mail: orders@knowres.co.za
Website: www.kr.co.za

Printed and bound: HartWood Digital Printing, 243 Alexandra Avenue, Halfway House, Midrand
Typesetting, layout and design: Cia Joubert, cia@knowres.co.za
Cover design: Marlene de'Lorme, marlene@knowres.co.za
Editing & proofreading: Valda Strauss, valda@global.co.za
Project management: Cia Joubert, cia@knowres.co.za
Index created with: TExtract/www.Texyz.com

Permissions Obtained:

   King Price:
   - Photographs: Ilze Claassen
   - Brand name: Marno Boshoff

   Missing Link:
   - Don Packett

   Illustrations:
   - Sandra Kellerman

   Author IP/Books:
   - Baumgartner, Jeffrey
   - Black, Robert Alan
   - Burkus, David
   - Fox Cabana, Olivia & Pollack, Judah
   - Gardner, Howard
   - Gelb, Michael, J.
   - Michalko, Michael

CREATIVE INTELLIGENCE
CQ@Play

Shaping your future in the Fourth
Industrial Revolution

Cherylene De Jager
With **Anton Muller**

2020

ACKNOWLEDGEMENTS

Thank you to everyone who has the courage to develop their Creative Intelligence (CQ). I hope that you will marvel at the magic of experiencing the AHA moment, that you will be brave enough to prototype these ideas and bold enough to apply them for everyone to optimally benefit from the proposed solutions.

I would like to thank Emeritus-Professor Anton Muller – your intellectual finesse and your linguistic mastery again places you in a league of your own. This project challenged on a different level. To those who agreed that I may use their Creative Intelligence (CQ) – you are thanked and acknowledged. To KR who agreed to publish the work – thank you for the opportunity to share my CQ with a broader audience. To Cia – you have the patience of a saint. To my husband, Johan, and my son, Andréas – words cannot begin to describe how much I appreciate your unconditional support.

May all of you who read this book discover what you are searching for and may unleashing your inner creative lead to roads not less travelled, but entirely new roads to be imagined, invented and created...

TABLE OF CONTENTS

ABOUT THE AUTHORS	iv
A WORD OR TWO	vi
CHAPTER 1: TRIGGERS & TRENDS	1
Why the renewed interest in creativity?	1
Reflections	20
CHAPTER 2: DETERMINANTS REQUIRED TO CREATE A CULTURE SUPPORTIVE OF CREATIVITY	21
What are the determinants required to create a culture supportive of creativity?	21
Reflections	37
CHAPTER 3: CREATIVE INTELLIGENCE (CQ)	39
Why CQ?	39
Reflections	46
CHAPTER 4: FUTURE SKILLS AND CREATIVITY	47
Why is creativity cited to be one of the top ten skills required to enable us to navigate the challenges posed by the 4IR?	47
Creativity Self-Test	52
Reflections	66
CHAPTER 5: IDEAS...	69
Where do ideas come from?	69
Reflections	74
CHAPTER 6: THE CREATIVE PROCESS	75
Does creativity just happen, or can it be willed/orchestrated/manipulated/controlled?	75
Reflections	78

CHAPTER 7: CREATIVITY TOOLKIT AND GRAB-PACK! 79

    Can CQ be developed through the use of methodologies, frameworks, techniques and tools? 79
    How to think like Leonardo da Vinci 81
    Divergent thinking and convergent thinking 83
    Divergent and Convergent Thinking explained… 84
    Divergent thinking exercises 87
    The Step-by-Step Guide to Brainstorming 94
    Brainstorming Exercises 96
    The Power of Play 107
    Reflections 108

CHAPTER 8: DESIGN THINKING 109

    Is Design Thinking merely a tool used to ignite creativity and innovation or is it a discipline in its own right? 109
    Design Thinking: A Twist on a Fairy Tale (or three) 113
    Reflections 116

CHAPTER 9: BREAKTHROUGH THINKING 119

    What do we need to know about breakthrough thinking? 119
    Reflections 128

CHAPTER 10: CQ(Creative Intelligence)@ PLAY… 129

    What is possible when CQ is @ play? 129
    Reflections 137

CHAPTER 11: REFLECTIONS… 139

    So where does this leave us? 139

A FINAL WORD OR TWO… 143

CREATIVITY SMORGASBORD…	**144**
Fifty thrifty thoughts about creativity…	144
INTENTIONS	**147**
What pearls of wisdom should you take from this book?	147
EPILOGUE	**149**
ENDNOTES	**151**
INDEX	**157**

ABOUT THE AUTHORS

Dr Cherylene de Jager is a creativity, innovation and change management specialist. Her impressive portfolio reflects a success story of more than twenty years. The multiple creativity, innovation and change journeys that she, in tandem with carefully selected associates, co-creates with high-profile clients and prominent South African and organisations in the rest of Africa, includes financial services organisations (Absa, Standard Bank, Nedbank), academic institutions (UJ, NWU), retail (Woolworths, Fochini), mining (Exarro; PPC), hospitality (Sun International) and construction companies (Grinaker-LTA). Music, mimes, magic, theatrical and interactive techniques, in tandem with sound change management methodologies, are used and participants find themselves totally immersed and engaged in the processes, whilst the strategic goals are achieved. Most importantly, the journey is legendary, exciting, extraordinary ... even dazzling! She owns the trademarks Corporate Cabaret® and Ideaneers® amongst others

She is a tenacious researcher and holds degrees focusing on change, creativity and innovation. She obtained a DPhil in Leadership in Performance and Change (one of the top ten students) from the University of Johannesburg, a Masters in Leadership in Performance and Change Management and BA Honours: Human Resource Development [cum laude) from the then Rand Afrikaans University and a BA(Ed) [cum laude] from the University of Pretoria. She is a published author and a sought-after speaker at high-profile functions. Her passion and purpose is to enhance the Creative Intelligence (CQ) of everyone she comes into contact with. Her manifesto is to add value, make a difference, create jobs and have fun while doing so.

Prof. Anton Muller retired in 2011 as Vice-Dean of the Faculty of Management with staff and student research and postgraduate studies as the main thrusts of his portfolio. He was also the research manager of the Faculty and chaired the Faculty Research Committee and the Faculty Higher Degrees Committee and he was a member of Manco. He served as a member of Senate and as a member of the institutional Higher

Degrees Committee and the Institutional Research Committee. In September 2011 he was appointed Emeritus Professor of the University of Johannesburg.

He commenced his studies at the University of the Witwatersrand obtaining the BA, BA Hons and Higher Education Diploma (Postgraduate). He then continued his studies at the Rand Afrikaans University where he obtained the B Ed (cum laude), the M Ed (cum laude) and the D Ed in 1989. His academic interests include, amongst others, higher education management, postgraduate research supervision, evaluation research, foreign language teaching, and educational technology. He is the author/co-author of some 180 plus outputs that include peer-reviewed journals, chapters in books, editor/co-editor of books, research reports, training modules, conference papers (national and international) and presentations to special interest groups. He supervised numerous doctoral and master's students. His personal interests include reading, the healing powers of crystals, jewellery making, painting/carving on linoleum and mosaic work. He still pursues some academic publishing with one of his past doctoral students, Dr Cherylene de Jager.

A WORD... OR TWO

All of us are born with an abundance of curiosity and creative potential. We started our journeys exploring and embracing the world with awe and our curiosity knew no boundaries. We approached everything without fear and with great enthusiasm. Our doting parents, grandparents, close family members and even family friends applauded everything we did (sometimes by just being polite when parents and grandparents showed off the new kid in the family with continuous wonder and pride) and encouraged us to try and try again until we got it right. Practice was the name of the game. We were not allowed to give up or to stop trying. Not getting it quite right was part of the learning curve.

Words were repeated over and over until we acquired and mastered the gift of speech. We were encouraged to walk and try again and again even though we fell and had to stand up and try again and again to finally master the act of walking. Every milestone we reached was celebrated. Our family and friends encouraged exploration and some of the people in our immediate circle re-discovered their own inner child when taking us to the zoo, the circus and various wonderlands. They marvelled at witnessing our joy when we clapped our hands and laughed (the imprinted accepted behaviours we learnt to express when experiencing joy) without restraint at the pure wonder of what life had to offer.

We at times displayed our artistic abilities by attempting to draw or write on walls and on furniture. The first couple of times even that behaviour was tolerated until social convention and proper conduct gently directed us to use paper, and if we were lucky, canvas and paint were available as the more appropriate options on which to showcase our budding artistic potential. We displayed our artistic efforts with confidence. Every effort was applauded, appreciated. We were encouraged to create more.

We started dressing up and some of us again were lucky enough to have grandmothers with trunks or suitcases full of old clothes and memorabilia that could be explored. We could create a world of make-believe and fantasy. Our imaginations had no boundaries. Some of us were fortunate enough to get hold of our mother or grandmother's make-up bag once or twice. Some of those encounters were encouraged and allowed us to further explore and indulge ourselves. Some were perhaps tolerated once or twice but then subtly, or at times maybe not so subtly, a couple of loving but firm boundaries were put in place. Well-intentioned parents always try at the very least to allow some degree of exploration and experimentation. I had the privilege to be in a family of musicians, artists and creative thinkers and tinkerers. My father and most of his family members played musical instruments. My father also enjoyed sketching and painting. None of them had the opportunity to practise their creative abilities professionally, but most of them enjoyed their creative pursuits as a hobby during weekends.

My fantasy world was further enhanced by a very doting and larger than life grandmother. My mother at the time allowed this indulgence and I will be forever grateful that the creative endeavours were observed, and even at times, encouraged. My grandmother made a fairy costume when I wanted to be a fairy. I am sure that I was the only fairy ever wearing a dainty blue fairy dress with silver wings and bottle-green clocks. My grandmother also made me a wonderful witch's costume when Liewe Heksie (a little South African witch with a heart of gold but with little flair and skill to get the spells right, and when she did, it was by pure accident and always just in time to save the day) first appeared as an animated cartoon character on South African TV. I could make mistakes and make them until I learnt from them.

I view myself as one of the lucky few to have had wonderful and creative early childhood development experiences. I couldn't wait for school to start. In those days most moms still stayed at home. We did not have pre-school as is the case today and grade one was our rite of passage into our scholastic careers. I arrived at school bright-eyed and bushy-tailed – ready to tackle this new adventure with gusto and an open-mind.

My mother's surprise was evident when I sent her home on the first day of school without as much as a tear or a sad face. I was more than ready to get started. We were given some wax crayons and a piece of paper with two circles on it. We were asked to colour in the circles. I decided that my circles would be blue and yellow. I chose yellow for the one circle and blue for the other. I then made zig-zag patterns with orange around the two circles once I was done filling the inside of the circles in with blue and yellow. I proudly went to the teacher's table to display my masterpiece when she called my name. That was my first experience with the reality of the education system: firstly, some of the blue and yellow colour was outside of the circle, and secondly, I did not strictly adhere to the instructions – the orange patterns around the circles were my first attempt at thinking outside of the box, in this case, outside of the circle.

 **Lesson number one: always colour within the lines and follow the instructions carefully. Do not be creative – do as you are told.**

I then started to colour within the lines as I was instructed to do. No more patterns or anything extra. A couple of days later my inner creative got the better of me and I chose the colour purple for Goldilocks' hair. The teacher was suitably mortified. She asked me what colour hair the other children in my class had. I was fortunate enough to know my colours well and said white (only later realising that white hair was referred to as being blonde), black and brown. She also asked me if any of them had purple hair. I answered that they did not but that some of my grandmother's friends had purple hair. Needless to say, my answer and initiative were not appreciated, and I was told to use yellow for the golden locks.

 **Lesson number two: do not use initiative or think out of the box – do what everybody else does and you will be fine.**

A few weeks later our teacher shared the story of Humpty Dumpty who sat on the wall and had a great fall. I wanted to engage in eager debate and dared to ask why an egg was sitting on a wall in the first place. I continued in spite of my teacher's astonished expression. With hindsight I thought her expression of horror at being questioned and challenged was one of wonder that I was so insightful (I did not have the level of EQ at the tender age of six to be able to differentiate expressions yet) as to know that eggs should either be eaten for breakfast on toast or be used to bake cakes. It was an oral assessment and I scored zero. Slowly but surely, I began to understand what the education system required of me. I learnt to masterfully navigate the system.

 **Lesson number three: do not question – memorise what was given to you and regurgitate it as is and you will be given high scores. What did Humpy Dumpty do? He sat on the wall and had a great fall – 100%. No questions, no debates.**

This behaviour dictated and directed the twelve years I spent at school. The first six months at university were a nightmare. I was fortunate enough to have English as a subject. There was a shortage of English teachers and bursaries were freely given by the Department of Education at the time to address these shortages. Horror of horrors – after years of merely memorising and reproducing information and content, I was asked to think, argue and produce original thought. I am still of the opinion that the gap between what is expected at schools and what is expected at universities is one of the major reasons why so many first-year students fail, drop out and battle to bridge the divide. It is better than thirty years ago, but the education system still has a long way to go to truly prepare the current generation for the challenges of the future world of work. More about that later.

I started my career as an English teacher. I taught at schools and I started to re-ignite and re-discover my latent creative potential. I could add my artistic flair and sense for the dramatic to my lessons in the classroom. I also directed and produced the school plays. I volunteered to be involved in fund-raising events for the schools where I taught. My entrepreneurial skills were developed. I will be forever grateful to those headmasters who were visionaries and created the environment for me to be able to express some of my passions and my dreams. Opportunities to experience the required 10 000 hours to master a variety of skills were ample.

I left teaching and spent a couple of years at tertiary institutions. I then started my consulting business. I started out as a change agent. I again had clients who wanted something different and creative. There was a slow but definite shift taking place in the passages of corporate South Africa. The conversation with regard to the need for innovation was ignited. The need for innovation evolved and is still relevant at present. The debates surrounding the concepts "innovation" and "creativity" are still alive and well. This begs the question: are creativity and innovation the same concepts or are they two different concepts? The one aspect that most people agree on is that both concepts are difficult to define. I have defined creativity as "the accomplishment of new developments as a result of the interaction between an individual and his/her environment with commercial intent". I have defined innovation as "the accomplishment of something new or the change of something that already exists, as a result of the interaction between an individual and his/her environment or a group with their environment with the sole purpose of commercial intent in the attempt to create wealth".

My view is that creativity precedes innovation and that innovation without creativity is sterile. I have defined the interrelatedness of the two concepts in the following way: "Innovation is creativity commercialised or even better, innovation is creativity in a business suit".

This begs the following questions: "What makes this book different from all the other books written about creativity?" and "Why another book about creativity and innovation?"

This book will not only focus on creativity and some elements of innovation but will shift the focus to Creative Intelligence (CQ), Creative Intelligence being a relatively new concept that still needs to be researched and explored. I have been involved with creativity research for more that fifteen years and I started to use the term CQ about ten years ago when I facilitated the section about the various intelligences. More about the intelligences later in the book. I have since bravely defined CQ: "Creative Intelligence (CQ) is knowing which methodologies, frameworks, techniques, tools and intelligences to use when, how and where to address client needs and to solve problems while imagining, inventing, creating and shaping the future". This book will also focus on and include South African examples where possible and applicable. The purpose of this book is to guide the reader through a process where the design of the book is informed by years of research and the practical application of the findings. The intent is to contextualise creativity in such a manner as to assist the reader to obtain an understanding of the current views with regard to creativity. The idea is also to include theoretical information and to foster an understanding of how to practically apply the acquired CQ (Creative Intelligence) should the opportunity present itself.

Leonardo da Vinci believed in making notes. **Keeping notes** or a diary is considered by thought leaders on creativity to be one of the most effective ways in which to explore ideas while on the quest of enhancing one's CQ (Creative Intelligence). The workbook should ideally be used as your personal CQ-developing notebook should the reader wish to do so. A separate notebook is advisable should the reader not wish to use this book as a workbook. The intent is to ignite the latent creative potential lurking within the reader. The focus will be on developing the CQ of the reader on a personal level as well as in an organisational context.

There is no right or wrong. Make mistakes. Learn from them. Move on. The idea is to experiment, to journey and to enjoy. Give yourself the gift of creative exploration and the permission to engage in discovering what the processes are all about with eager anticipation. Then attempt to apply them in the workplace. Think about ways in which to obtain an added benefit from the process by assisting your team members to develop their CQ. Share the gift of creative exploration with your team members. Take the cognitive decision to be mindful, to be present in the moment. Embrace the journey, enjoy the process. You can apply these methodologies, frameworks, techniques and tools in your professional as well as in your personal life. The only limitations are self-imposed. Give yourself permission to break free and to liberate your mainframe.

Some people are fortunate enough to discover their purpose and calling early on in their lives. It took me years and many a detour to eventually discover mine. My purpose, passion and my calling are to enhance the CQ of everyone I have the joy of meeting and to introduce them to creative and innovative thinking and problem-solving skills enabling them to contribute to changing the world for the betterment of humankind.

The content and exercises in this book can assist individuals to obtain an understanding of creativity while at the same time allowing them to work through the methodologies, frameworks, techniques and tools that will enhance and develop their CQ.

The book starts by providing the reader with a brief overview of the triggers and trends that ignite creativity. This is followed by a discussion about which determinants on an organisational as well as on an individual level are required to establish an environment supportive of creativity and innovation. Creative Intelligence is then introduced and contextualised. An overview is then given about what to consider regarding future skills requirements followed by a more comprehensive discussion of creativity. Creativity is an important component of CQ. The methodologies, frameworks, techniques and tools that enhance creativity are for the time being those employed to enhance CQ. CQ is knowing which methodologies, frameworks, techniques and tools to utilise when, where and how.

The aim is to use these methodologies, frameworks, techniques and tools to generate as many creative ideas as possible. Ideaneering, ideation or idea-generation is part of the creative process. A short overview of the creative process is given. This is followed by a comprehensive creativity toolkit or grab-pack. Design thinking is unpacked and some fun exercises will stretch your imagination. Now that your imagination is suitably stretched, you are ready to read more about how breakthrough thinking occur.

It is now time to provide some practical examples of CQ@play for you to explore and ponder. Some global and local examples are shared. The book concludes with some mega reflections, a creativity smorgasboard, a list of good intentions to cultivate and an epilogue that will leave you with some food for thought.

A few more inspirational thoughts:

- Make the decision to improve your CQ (if you are reading this you already have)
- Then get started (one simple exercise a day)
- Take action (just do it)
- You do not need to know it all at once (one step at a time)

The design of this book includes methodologies, frameworks, techniques and tools aimed at enhancing and developing your CQ. One of these techniques is to combine different elements. The design of this book combines elements of storytelling, academic theories and practical examples. Conversational paragraphs are interrupted or supported by academic theories and facts. Different writing styles are used. Sometimes the information is conveyed in the form of a narrative; at other times it is merely given as a list of bullet-points, or mini-case studies. At times examples are given and sometimes a mere picture paints a 1 000 words.

Now have the liquid temptation of your choice close by and enjoy the experience!

Whatever creativity is, it is in part a solution to a problem.

Brian Aldiss

Chapter 1

Triggers & Trends

Why the renewed interest in creativity?

Various external triggers ranging from the socio-economic and political environment, namely unexpected outside events such as the global economic challenges, new regulatory and statutory requirements, unexpected competition from rivals, increasingly demanding customer expectations and the unknown challenges posed by the Fourth Industrial Revolution (4IR), resulted in the realisation that organisations have to become more creative and innovative in order to secure future sustainability. Creativity is listed on various future-skills lists as being one of the top ten skills required to successfully navigate the challenges posed by the Fourth Industrial Revolution (4IR). What is meant by the 4IR? The first IR was ignited by the discovery of steam, the second IR by electricity and the third IR by the digital (computers and technology) revolution. The Fourth Industrial Revolution is the current and developing environment in which disruptive technologies and trends such as the Internet of Things (IoT), robotics, virtual reality (VR), 3D printing and artificial intelligence (AI) are changing the way we live and work. The 4IR is a combination and fusion of technologies blurring the lines between the physical, digital and biological spheres. The 4IR makes the other three revolutions look like child's play.

> The Fourth Industrial Revolution is transformative in nature. It requires constant creative solutions and problem-solving capabilities to create and shape a future veiled in uncertainty.

The 4IR impacts societies, communication, learning and business. The aging of the Baby Boomer generation and the rise of Gen Y poses its own challenges. Gen Y's stronger embrace of sustainability, same-sex marriages and racial and ethnic integration as a result of having been born into a world where such cultural values are more widely accepted is affecting not only those born after 1980 but nations holistically. Gen Y's desire to participate in and create their own media, online personas and communication models impacts societies, communication, learning and the world of work. Social media's rise has drastically altered industries from journalism to health care, altering virtually everything we do and how we do it. **The future is now. We are already partly living in a digitised world.** Facebook, LinkedIn, Instagram and Spotify all use technology that allows people to directly build and organise their own communities in flat, horizontal and more democratic ways. We find and create our own tribes and communities where we are accepted, celebrated and welcomed. This is an extreme departure from the ways of how it was traditionally done. Organisations, schools, hospitals and virtually all aspects of our lives need to adapt to social technology – or be replaced.

Some of the main effects of the looming changes on business impacts customer expectations, product enhancement, collaborative innovation and organisational forms/structures. The solution posed by business: EVERYONE MUST INNOVATE! In the seventies, the bikini was the solution to it all – if you want to sell something, place it next to a lady in a bikini. Innovation seems to have become the bikini of the 21st century. The debate regarding the terms "innovation" and "creativity" is still pending. Potato versus potato or potato versus tomato or is it merely a matter of "a rose by any other name?" My view resonates with those who argue that innovation without creativity is sterile, and some argue, even impossible. My view is that creativity precedes innovation. The definition that I eventually coined and one that has been cited in a list containing top innovation quotes is: "INNOVATION IS CREATIVITY COMMERCIALISED".

Creativity cannot be explored in isolation. There is an interrelatedness and a close correlation to innovation, design thinking and change. There is also an interplay between the individual, the team or teams in which the individual operates and the organisation or environment. The culture of the organisation is also a factor that must be taken into consideration.

The speed of technological breakthroughs, the scope, the scale and complexity thereof and the impact of the new systems resulted in inventions that are currently creating a New World of Work (NWOW) while at the same time shaping societies and transforming cities. Design is required and never have creativity and innovation been so important. The reality of these rapid changes is that there will in all likelihood be job losses, but other jobs will be created, for example, operating and controlling drones transporting medicine and take-aways, monitoring cars and trucks without drivers, overseeing robots making food and instructing and training people on how to behave in people-free supermarkets and restaurants.

The new jobs that are created will be powered by creativity. The way in which organisations need to train and equip their workforce, by necessity, will also have to change. This shift in the workforce has meant a major change in desired skills from 2015 – 2020, a massive shift in just five years. Desired skills are shifting from coordinating with others and active listening to things like **complex problem solving, critical thinking and creativity.** Organisations need a way to design training in such a way that it develops these skills and competencies while it fits into the modern learner's busy schedules and at the same time creates real behaviour change.

It appears that training and instruction of new protocols and processes could be your next career option to consider. The above will require new protocols, governance and legislation. Integrity and ethics will be more important than ever before in the history of humankind. A new code of cyber-chivalry needs to emerge and evolve.

I was recently asked to address a group of top achievers at an awards ceremony. The delegate profile consisted mostly of aspiring medical doctors and engineers. The achievers attending this award ceremony scored an average of 80% or higher in either maths, physics or chemistry. Some of them even scored 100% in maths. I conducted some research and the impact of the 4IR, still in its infancy, on some of the breakthroughs in the health and education sectors, is simply mind-altering.

Health and education – all humans should have access to both – will still exist but both industries have already begun to evolve rapidly and will be very different in future. In the health industry new knowledge of the brain, its potential and how it operates is rapidly expanding due to the creation of a machine that visualises brain activity. Neuroscience is making rapid strides in understanding how the brain works. The idea is that machines must be utilised to augment our innate capacities for the better. A cure for paralysis is being researched where machines are used to assist patients who are paralysed. The first experiments are already being conducted. Fatty tissue is extracted, stem cells are removed, and a process has been developed that can create living bone ready for transplant.

The impact on health care is just as impressive. Creative and innovative ways of bringing the cost down are explored and health care will hopefully become more cost effective and more accessible to everyone. The industry aims to explore more, better and faster ways to bring medicine to clients and drones are already being used to take medicine to remote areas. New ways of record keeping are explored whereby a doctor's ability to manage sickness is improved. The doctor will be able to better predict a patient's condition and will be able to personalise healthcare solutions. Data will assist medical practitioners to measure more accurately and to provide better solutions. Virtual Reality can create a hologram for surgeons to practise the surgical procedure before the actual surgery is performed.

The focus will be more on the patient and preventative care. Patients will become active in managing their own health. The patient will be part of the decision-making. It is not a one-sided affair anymore. The doctor–patient relationship will become one of collaboration. Hospital care will be extended to your own home. Certain sleeves have been developed that monitor certain conditions and functions. Patients will become more involved in managing their own health and will take ownership of their physical well-being. There are, however, numerous challenges remaining and researchers still hope to find a cure for cancer, reduce obesity and prevent diabetes and heart attacks.

Again, issues remain to be resolved and to be addressed but imagine the possibilities and impact of providing cost-effective and accessible health care to not only everyone in South Africa, but also everyone in Africa, or for that matter, in the world.

The face of education will change forever. The influence of Google, Wikipedia and YouTube on learning must not be underestimated. Content must be short and to the point and not TLTR (Too Long To Read). The impact on learning retention, the transfer of learning and the application of learning is yet to be determined. Learning styles (PART – Pragmatists, Activists, Reflectors and Theorists) and technology will have to evolve in tandem enabling people to optimally learn faster than ever before in order to remain competitive. A question that is still frequently asked is: How does learning take place in the brains of students? Or for that matter: How do we learn? Some of these questions will be addressed in the course of the book.

Literature traditionally features the brain as the basis of learning, memory, knowledge, even reading and mathematics but there is almost no mention of education, schools or classrooms. There is mixed reaction to the emergence of educational neuroscience. A brief overview of neuroscience and the impact on creativity will be given at a later stage. There is an urgent need for the education profession to share a professionally uniform educational neuroscience research agenda for the future. One of the many questions that teachers can put on the neuroscience research agenda is: Why do some children learn more easily than others?

Our current education system is based on an outdated model rooted in the late 19th century. It is driven by archaic pedagogic practices and old-fashioned textbooks and is measured, as referred to in the beginning of this book, by the mere reproduction of facts rather than design. There is inadequate accommodation of or appreciation for original thought or creativity in any form at all. The education system may have envisioned that this form of teaching will eventually evolve to where computers replace teachers. This view and vision completely misunderstood the unique nature of teaching and learning. In its ideal form, teaching and learning is a uniquely personal interaction between educators and scholars where the interaction should cater to every learner's changing needs, budding talents, pace of learning, passions and interests. In fact, the very skills required to still differentiate human learners from the machines that are now emerging as part of this next industrial revolution.

Alvin Toffler in his book, *Future Shock*, in 1970 stated that "The illiterate of the 21st century will not be those who cannot read and write, but those who cannot learn, unlearn and relearn."[1] The pace of having to be able to navigate through this cycle has accelerated exponentially. Education, and the manner in which we learn, need to be totally re-designed in order to equip the current, as well as the future workforce, with the necessary skills to not only navigate the challenges posed by the 4IR but to also co-create and thrive in a world not yet imagined. There are numerous lists as to what skills will be required in future.[2]

Some of the future skills required are:

Creativity	the future world of work is going to demand new ways of thinking and human creativity is the key to do it
Emotional Intelligence	machines do not have empathy and can't easily replace a human's ability to connect with another human being, so those with a high EQ will be in demand
Critical Thinking	the future will require people who will rely on logical reasoning rather than emotion, weigh the options carefully and consider the best possible solution; people with strong analytical thinking will be needed to navigate the human/machine division of labour
Active learning with a can-do mindset	people with such a mindset know that their intelligences and abilities can be developed and they know their effort to build skills will result in higher achievement. They will take on new challenges, learn from mistakes, and actively seek new knowledge

Judgement and decision making	as technology takes away more menial and mundane tasks, it will leave humans free to do more higher-level decision making
Interpersonal communication skills	the ability to exchange information and meaning between people will be a vital skill during the 4IR
Leadership skills	leadership traits such as inspiring others and helping people to become the best versions of themselves will be necessary for the future workforce
Diversity and cultural intelligence	it is vital that individuals have the skills to understand, respect and work with others despite differences in race, culture, language, age, gender, sexual orientation, political and religious beliefs, to name but a few
Technology skills	the 4IR is fuelled by innovations such as AI, big data, virtual reality, blockchain, robotics and more; and this means that everyone will need a certain level of comfort or ease around technology; some degree of technical skills (digital literacy); and understanding the potential impact of new technologies on their industry, business and jobs
Embracing change	due to the speed of change in the future workplace, people will have to be agile and be able to embrace and celebrate change; we need to be able to adjust to shifting workplaces, expectations and skillsets – an essential skill during the 4IR will be the ability to see change as an opportunity to grow and to innovate

Creative Intelligence (CQ)	creativity is an important component of CQ; CQ is knowing how to unleash the creative potential of individuals and teams by utilising methodologies, frameworks, techniques and tools to mine their prior knowledge, to **create a learn-while-you-play and play-while-you-learn mindset,** create prototypes and bring the ideas to market while constantly re-imagining, re-inventing and re-creating a new world – CQ the ability to integrate and select the above skills and utilise them optimally in the appropriate contexts

Designing learning experiences that encourage learners to make things by collaboratively solving real-world challenges will be the key to thriving in this century. Education within the developing world is still to a large degree based on repetitive learning rather than on a creativity-based curriculum. The school system by and large still focuses on "cognitive intelligence" and aims at developing abilities and skills measured by IQ (Intelligence Quotient). Inert (meaning unable to move) intelligence is what you demonstrate when you take an IQ test, or a similar test used for university or graduate school admissions. High scores on a test measuring inert intelligence don't guarantee success. Measurement at schools and university still to a large degree relies on a system where learners are required to recall facts. Learners who can recall facts, even reason with them, don't necessarily know how to utilise and apply these facts to add value or make a difference. Creativity in education in the United States of America was a topic of urgent discussion in schools during the 1960s and was triggered by the Russian launch of Sputnik.

> In South Africa the realities of the current educational system and the challenges it faces have triggered the need for a focus on creativity in schools.

The challenges South Africa faces with regard to youth employment further emphasise the need for a renewed focus on creativity not only in schools, but creativity across the entire spectrum impacted by the 4IR. There is a call to business, an appeal, to participate in the design of an intervention to address youth unemployment. The question to address is: "How are the employees of tomorrow preparing for the 4IR, and subsequent revolutions, today?" and "Who is responsible for preparing them?" The Deloitte paper on preparing tomorrow's workforce for the 4IR suggests the following:[3]

- The intervention design needs to work with the broader ecosystem and the designers must strive to align stakeholder objectives and approaches

- Business should strategically engage in public policy through dialogue, collaboration and influence

- Business must ideally develop promising talent strategies with a focus on youth

- Business should invest strategically in workforce training approaches and should strive to align workforce training programmes with their strategic goals, talent practices, skills needs and corporate culture

What will be our saving grace in an era where technological change is more exponential and more rapid than our ability to change? We will have to become change fit. A small consolation for the time being is that machines do not have empathy. They can recognise empathy, but they do not have it. Machines are also not capable of critical thinking. They do not yet have critical thought. Machines cannot yet imagine. Machines are not creative. Cultivating a mind-set for lifelong learning and consciously improving your CQ (Creative Intelligence) will help you to cope during this transitional period between revolutions. You will acquire the ability to solve problems and pro-actively co-create a future by being able to creatively connect the dots. This will prepare you for the skills required for the future. Creativity and CQ will be sought after skills for the 4IR. This brings me back to the topic of creativity.

Creativity has long been viewed as the exclusive domain of writers, artists, musicians and actors. The good news is that there has been a shift in thinking from creativity being an attribute of a fortunate few to one that everyone is creative, and that creativity can be developed. We are born with the ability to create. When we are young, we constantly explore our creative potential and we regularly exercise our creative muscle. An ordinary stick becomes a fishing rod, a sword, a magic wand, a telescope. Then we go to school and we are forced to colour between the lines. University follows and the first-year failure rates are still shocking. Our education system consists of schools traditionally teaching students to memorise and repeat and not to think critically or creatively.

At university some degree of creative thinking and practical application is required. The theory in some cases is still far removed from reality. Traditionally, creativity was further stifled at work. People in creative professions were in some instances merely tolerated or viewed as being weird. They at least had the luxury of being allowed to be creative at work. There has been a definite shift in the past couple of years as to how the value of critical thinking, imagination, the ability to generate new ideas and creativity are viewed in organisations. Recruiters now in all earnest look for and source candidates who display those skills.

The workplace spaces and offices of some organisations have been transformed to display this new approach and trend. The New World of Work (NWOW) requires from us to be more creative and innovative than ever before in history. Creativity and the ability to navigate the technology changes posed by the 4IR will give organisations the competitive edge to not only survive but to thrive while creating a NWOW.

A new kind of quest for talent is in the making: **The quest for talent whose CQ is sufficiently developed to enable them to navigate their ogranisations through the 4IR and beyond.** Organisations need to creatively engage in the design of unique CX (Customer Experiences), UX (User Experiences), DX (Digital Experiences) and then design a workable TX (Transformational Experience) to assist the customer to embrace the changes introduced by the 4IR.

An attempt to address the latter was manifested in the expectation of organisations that everyone must innovate. The development of creative and innovative thinking skills is crucial for the survival of organisations in the twenty-first century. The realisation that in times of increasing global competition and rapidly increasing change the need exists for managers and

Chapter 1: Triggers & Trends

leaders to be able to respond in ways not previously imagined. An organisation's ability to innovate will afford it the competitive advantage it requires to survive. Creativity of individuals and teams can be developed by acquiring and utilising creative thinking and problem-solving methodologies, frameworks, techniques and tools. Creativity and original thought ensure competitive advantage. Constantly improving the Creative Intelligence (CQ) of the current as well as the future workforce is not an option anymore, but a necessity. Enhancing the Creative Intelligence (CQ) of the current as well as the future workforce can shape a society to improve the collective creative and innovative thinking and problem-solving skills and co-create a future where everyone will thrive.

The infographic that follows provides a high-level overview of the elements @ play in the 4IR.

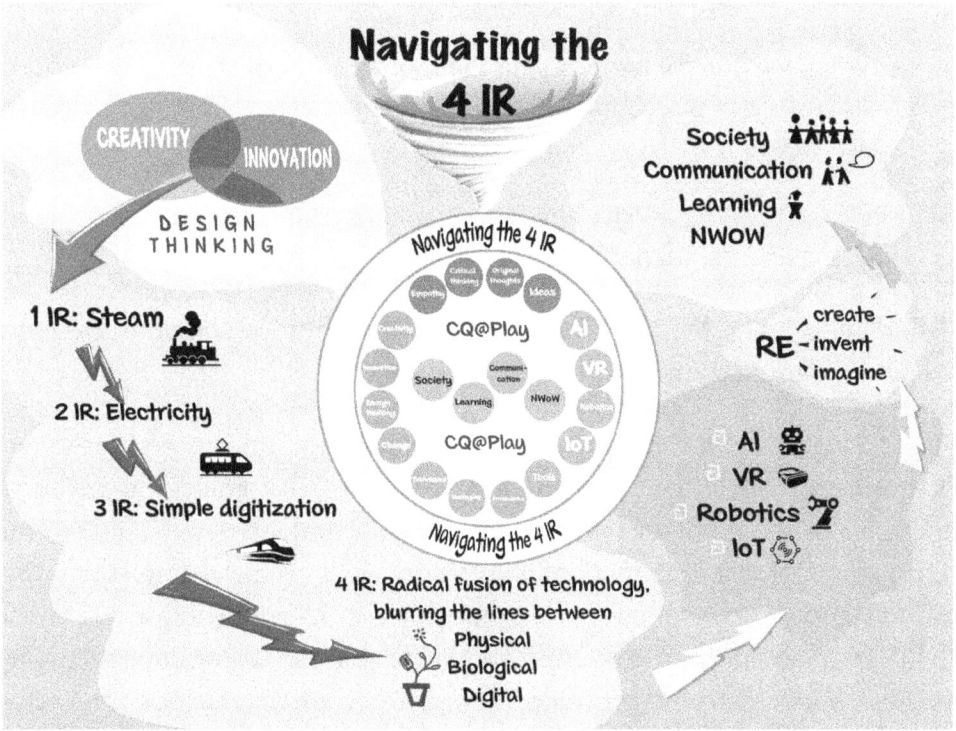

Figure 1: Navigating the 4 IR (Design: C. de Jager. Illustration: Sandra Kellerman)

A few last points to ponder:

- Youth employment and youth skills development initiatives are some of the salient issues to navigate as the 4IR's impact is becoming more and more evident in all spheres of our lives. One solution of how to address this challenge is for the business community to employ a youth corporate strategy to leverage diverse perspectives that can drive innovation and creativity.

- Intellectual Property (IP) rights online and in a digital world will have to be re-looked, re-visited and debated

- Biohacking requires some serious debates, thoughts and regulations

- Artificial Intelligence (AI) is not yet fully understood or controlled – **What can/could go wrong?** – a valid question without a clear and definitive answer

- Your knowledge will be obsolete the moment you graduate – one of the real challenges faced by our current educational system and the way in which we learn

- Life-long learning which implies constant upskilling and re-skilling should become an integral part of our daily lives

Trends also ignite the need for creative and innovative solutions. How do trends influence creativity?

Rapid advances in technology and the creative application thereof resulted in business models that addressed the needs of customers and changed the rules of the game of the industry in which they operate. Think Airbnb (the world's largest accommodation provider owns no real estate), Uber (the world's largest taxi company owns no vehicles), Alibaba (the world's most valuable retailer has no inventory) and Facebook (the world's most popular media owner creates no content). They have broken and changed the rules of the game without destroying traditional business models by creating new business models. What will be next?

Nussbaum states that indications are that almost 50% of the American workforce will be freelancers by 2020 and beyond.[4] These portfolio workers so-called are referred to as nomads. The world of work will have to adjust its policies and views to accommodate this nomad workforce. This trend is evident in Rosebank, South Africa, where a workspace called Perch provides infrastructure to nomad workers and they are managed by a group appropriately calling themselves: Nomads. **This goes to show that the future is already here.**

Nussbaum[5] mentions the making culture and identified the value-add of the wanderers. The arrival and the increasing popularity of a 'Making Culture' are of enormous importance and have far-reaching consequences. For a generation, we have outsourced making, but now, a lot of countries are bringing it home. Lower-cost making technologies, such as 3-D printing, crowd-funding and social media and a switch in values are combining to mark a shift from globalisation to localisation. In South Africa the market-making culture ranges from regular markets such as the Rosebank Rooftop Market, the Bryanston Organic Market which operates on a weekly basis and the Linden Market which operates quarterly in Gauteng to pop-up markets at various shopping centres. Several festivals and markets across South Africa provide opportunities for the "makers" to display their skills and sell their crafts. The concept of markets is not new – the revived interest in them is.

Another trend Nussbaum[6] mentioned is the utilisation of the so-called "wanderers". What are "wanderers", and how can they help leverage creative solutions? Wanderers are people on the 'outside' who can detect, appreciate and spot new ideas, decide what has the best chance of success, and provide financing or connections to make it happen. In art, there is the gallery owner; in music, the producer; in sports, the coach and in theatre the producer/director.

Impact of the 4IR on South Africa in particular has shifted the focus to the following areas. Data, and especially data analysis, has received major attention. The trend is to collect and analyse vast amounts of data and the patterns and insights obtained will form the backbone of future business. Data-driven decisions will be the key to success and adopting a "data-first" mindset will therefore be essential for future success.

Increasing connectivity is taking globalisation to an entirely new level. Businesses can reach a wider audience than ever before. Training is done via platforms such as Zoom, BlueJeans and Skype for Business. Companies should be encouraged to adopt an international mindset. The secret to being able to successfully navigate the 4IR is to continuously develop your workforce. Businesses should make sure that their workforce has the required level of technical skills. But the focus should not just be on technical skills.

> Software is taking over most of the mundane, time-consuming tasks, therefore human skills such as creativity, critical thinking, problem solving, and communication will be key to the workforce of the future.

Developing your workforce is not enough. Organisations should take into consideration how the workforce is currently evolving. The workplace is more diverse than at any other time in history. A diverse workforce, thriving on social collaboration augmented by technology is re-defining the world-of-work and the manner in which we communicate. Individual power is stronger than ever before and today employees are with a company because they choose to be there. **Creating a "human experience" in the workplace is the need of the hour.** There are numerous factors that drive the needs of employees. Organisations need to understand these changing needs in order to meet the aspirations of their future employees

Career aspirations, work–life and lifestyle balance are important considerations when selecting an employer. Careers will be a series of events – non-linear and unpredictable. The current work reality is that employees must keep their skillsets relevant. Employees seek growth and developmental opportunities to maintain competitive skillsets. They are actively seeking challenging projects, new roles and unique experiences that offer an opportunity to learn and grow both personally (soft skills, thought processes) and professionally (capability, knowledge). The current and future workforce should be made aware that their learning agility will enhance their performance and fast-track their careers. They need to become active and life-long learners and they must pursue various knowledge sources. They need to become change-fit, knowledge-hungry and find a way in which to rapidly and continually build new skillsets.

Employees who have discovered their purpose, passion and the value-add of their work will optimally perform while making a difference. Career paths and succession planning as we know them will soon be relics of the past. Lifetime employment will in all probability soon be a fond memory of how things used to be done in the corporate corridors. Employees will find new ways in which to add value and assess the impact of their contributions to their teams, functions, departments and organisations.

Corporate cultures and behaviours need to find ways that will enable employees to experience a sense of belonging. A culture of respect and inclusion will assist the individual to feel that they "fit in". A culture where the individual feels safe will encourage the individual to share freely and the organisation gains from this cognitive contribution and diversity. Employees who feel safe will also offer their ideas freely. The culture must also allow for making mistakes and learning from them. Humans have a need to collaborate and collaboration ignites ideas.

There is a need for personalisation. More personalised, agile and holistic recognition and rewards agreements are the trend. The pay-check is still essential and fair pay symbolises respect and appreciation for their contribution. The impact of the long hours and accompanying stress on the social and emotional well-being of the workforce and their productivity must be acknowledged. Work–life balance and the juggling of priorities are in some ways made easier by the way in which technology facilitates communication and planning. People need to feel psychologically safe in the workplace and they must be able to be themselves. Diverse lifestyle choices need to be respected. Diverse backgrounds contribute to the expression of different points of views. This level of cognitive diversity benefits organisations and creates a fertile breeding ground for creativity.

Employees must adopt an agile mindset and recognise the importance of agility and flexibility. Adapt to the fast pace of change. Become change-fit. Culture must be geared towards productivity and agility to enhance the customer experience which in turn should result in more sales.

The current workforce is in flux and individuals as well as organisations are trying to design solutions as to how to creatively navigate this transition phase. The preparation and skills development of the future workforce should also be taken into consideration. Therefore certain trends in the education arena must be noted.

One should take note of the following trends in the South African education arena. There is a stronger focus on private HE (Higher Education) providers who can provide **blended learning options** which offer distance, online and some face-to-face learning interaction should it be required. This will assist to prepare the future workforce for the evolving learning and development model that is currently taking shape. The impact of the economic and political realities, the changing requirements of the academic profession, the evolution of the teaching and learning curricula and the need to create and design new ways of how to learn, unlearn and re-learn cannot be ignored by the education sector.

Online learning will assist to address the need for quality education in a country that is unable to build universities to cater to the rate of population growth. The impact of AI demands the need to develop a technology-savvy future workforce. Using AI will change the way learners proceed to internalise, transfer and apply knowledge. It is estimated that more than 80% of all future jobs will require STEM (science, technology, engineering and maths) education. The South African government in tandem with industry and other role players are trying their best to begin to address these shortfalls. The need for flexible delivery modes requires HEI's to consider different modes of delivery in order to maximise student success.

Sub-Saharan Africa is experiencing rapid growth with the demand for education outstripping supply. Numerous students from Sub-Saharan Africa choose to study in SA.

The reality is that a very insignificant number of public schools in SA use technology to enhance teaching and learning. The current education system is still far from utilising technology to open the doors of learning and make education accessible to all, as envisaged in the country's constitution.

Decolonisation of the curriculum is a process of institutionally embodying the theoretical, historical, literary, artistic, other forms of expression and experiences of other indigenous people. There is growing consensus amongst social scientists and public administration practitioners about the importance of decolonising the education system in Africa and South Africa. The transformation of the curriculum remains a challenge with questions of how decolonisation or transformation is to be conceptualised, delineated and implemented. This challenge remains unanswered and unresolved.[7, 8]

The magic of Africa will be reflected – African Magic requires that African talent and brands are showcased as being up there with the best in class. If you are a brand, a creative or entrepreneur in Africa, now is your time to shine. For Western brands and entrepreneurs, partnership with African Magic is essential. The Serpentine Galleries in London appointed Burkina Faso's Francis Kéré to design its annual temporary park pavilion in July 2017.[9]

The Citizen Woke trend inspires the business case for why global brands must strive to decolonise consumerism. Brands need to acknowledge the African heritage and celebrate the nuances of the markets being served and ultimately decolonise consumption. Jameson's, the Irish Whisky brand, celebrated Nigeria's Independence Day with a free event called "Jameson Connects Nigeria". The event celebrated Nigeria's history and culture with traditional food and palm-wine cocktails, and was held at the Old Running Shed, which houses Lagos' oldest train relics. These are but a few selected examples.

Smart technology is reaching its tipping point across the continent and will promote the rise of the Smart Market. AI, VR, IoTs, Robotics, 3D-printing … the list goes on. In short, as the rest of the world tinkers with breakthrough solutions that will push humanity into a new phase of innovation and technological advancement, Africa represents a region where the smart technology game is yet to truly take flight. The lives of many Africans remain untouched by intelligent, automated infrastructure. However, driven by increased smartphone adoption, falling internet costs, a growing entrepreneurial scene, a surge in start-up funding and ground-breaking investments in the tech-ecosystem, the time may be ripe for the continent to finally leapfrog into smarter technological solutions. Through The Internet of Life the horns of black rhinos (classified as a critically endangered species) were equipped with internet-connected sensors in September 2017. The Internet of Life's initiative is part of the Smart Park programme to protect wildlife in Africa through technology. It is successfully used in Tanzania to prevent poaching.[10]

Social media definitely impact trends and here is an overview of the some of the future marketing trends to be aware of. One of the major trends is the rise of the social CEO. Customers want "real" brand stories and they want to know what drives them. Leaders who are successful on social media show their companies' human side and give their brands credibility and personality. This builds loyalty and, in some cases, an emotional connection that goes beyond the product or service. Share stories that demonstrate your leadership style as well as company culture.

While 2018 brought a renewed focus on the utilisation of chatbots, the trend for 2019 is really using the bots to gather information about consumers by engaging with them on a personal level and steering them towards a sale. The current trends include the utilisation of bots to transport medicine, blood and documents. Facebook Messenger becomes more and more useful for brands as the platform allows customisation of automated messages and the ability to initiate a conversation at the right time. You can also integrate this with Facebook shopping and increase conversion rates by enabling the bot to sell products to a consumer through the Facebook platform.

Keep it local. Try to identify and partner with local influencers that are happy to work on long-term campaigns. Also use multiple touch points including podcasts, YouTube, Snapchat and Instagram. Before you reach out to an influencer, follow them and learn a bit about the way they represent brands and engage with their fans to see if they'll be a good fit.

Personalise email communication. Make sure to use automation and personalisation to really make your customers feel that you are listening. Use automated campaigns after a first purchase, to request a review on social platforms, or just thank customers for shopping and remind them to share their purchase online.

Post in real time. To incorporate offline marketing into the online world, Instagram TV or IGTV allows brands to create a place for consumers to watch live events or brand content in their own time.

Whatever trends come our way or happen to unfold and evolve, the key is to remain agile and adapt to how customers engage with your brand. And more than ever before, it's important for all marketing touch points to align and communicate the same message.

Internet retailing begins to grow and drive online shopping. Smartphones will further drive online shopping growth. Consumers gravitate to social media and this resulted in consumers increasingly engaging with brands online. This in turn ignites creative marketing strategies and brands re-inventing their identities and online presence.[11]

Triggers and trends shape the 4IR and inspire creativity and innovation. The correct environment must ideally be created to enable individuals to access their creative potential and to optimally put it to play.

Reflections

- Be aware of rapid advances in technology and the application thereof
- Take notice what the industry game changers do
- Be aware of the workforce composition: the nomads and the freelancers
- Note the return of the making culture and the value-add of the wanderers
- Take note of the buzz around data
- Collaborate and consciously try to connect the dots
- Utilise the emergence of individual power
- Understand the impact of the talent wars
- Embrace the culture of inclusion
- Cultivate an agile mindset
- Assess the return of personalisation
- Chanel the impact of social media
- Monitor the impact of online shopping
- The impact of technology-induced change on societies, communities, learning and the world of work requires people to be more creative and innovative than ever before
- This new world requires that a new code of ethics, new legislation and a degree of cyber-chivalry needs to be developed
- Empathy, being change-fit, embracing life-long learning and being able to think critically, solve problems and creativity, to mention but a few, will ensure your competitive advantage
- Current jobs may become obsolete but new jobs will create exciting opportunities
- We need to acquire the skills to navigate an uncertain and evolving future utilising creativity and CQ to design that future…

Closer to home:

- Private HE providers
- Youth unemployment
- Decolonisation of Africa

Chapter 2

Determinants Required to Create a Culture Supportive of Creativity

What are the determinants required to create a culture supportive of creativity?

The **environment** plays a crucial role in enhancing creativity. The interaction between the individual and his/her environment is essential for him/her to be creative. Florence produced great painters such as Leonardo da Vinci, Raphael, Botticelli and Donatello amongst others. Is it coincidence or were there some other determinants at play? Florence at the time was a very rich city and the elite marked their status by acquiring art. Artists thus flocked to Florence to capitalise on the prevailing opportunities. They collaborated and they sought each other's advice and criticism. The cultural and social context in Florence at the time was supportive of creativity. Art and creativity thrived due to the right mix of political and economic conditions. Those conditions sadly no longer exist in Florence and the current creative output reflects that. Just as the prevailing conditions in a country or city influence creative output, the same can be said in an organisational context.

An environment that promotes creativity is not an automatic process but should be actively created by the owners and/or leaders of organisations. Such an environment is characterised by trust, openness, the existence of humour and the comfort to be able to debate issues. There should be enough resources and freedom to achieve creative results.

Leaders and managers can improve their organisation's creative climate. They should encourage creativity and it is therefore important that management know how to change their organisation's culture so that their employees learn to think more creatively. Certain organisational determinants need to be in place in order to establish a culture supportive of creativity.

The current reality of the extent to which the existing determinants are supportive of creativity and the level of CQ in the organisation need to be assessed. This in turn will inform the scope of the intervention to be designed when organisations realise that enhancing the CQ of their employees to equip them to be able to navigate the challenges posed by the 4IR is not an option, but a vital requirement/necessity. The more supportive the current organisational determinants are of creativity and the higher the level of CQ of the individuals, the less intense the scope of the actions or remedies to be taken.

Figure 2 illustrates the determinants that are required to establish a culture supportive of creativity – a traditional and conventional perspective.[12]

Chapter 2: Determinants Required to Create a Culture Supportive of Creativity

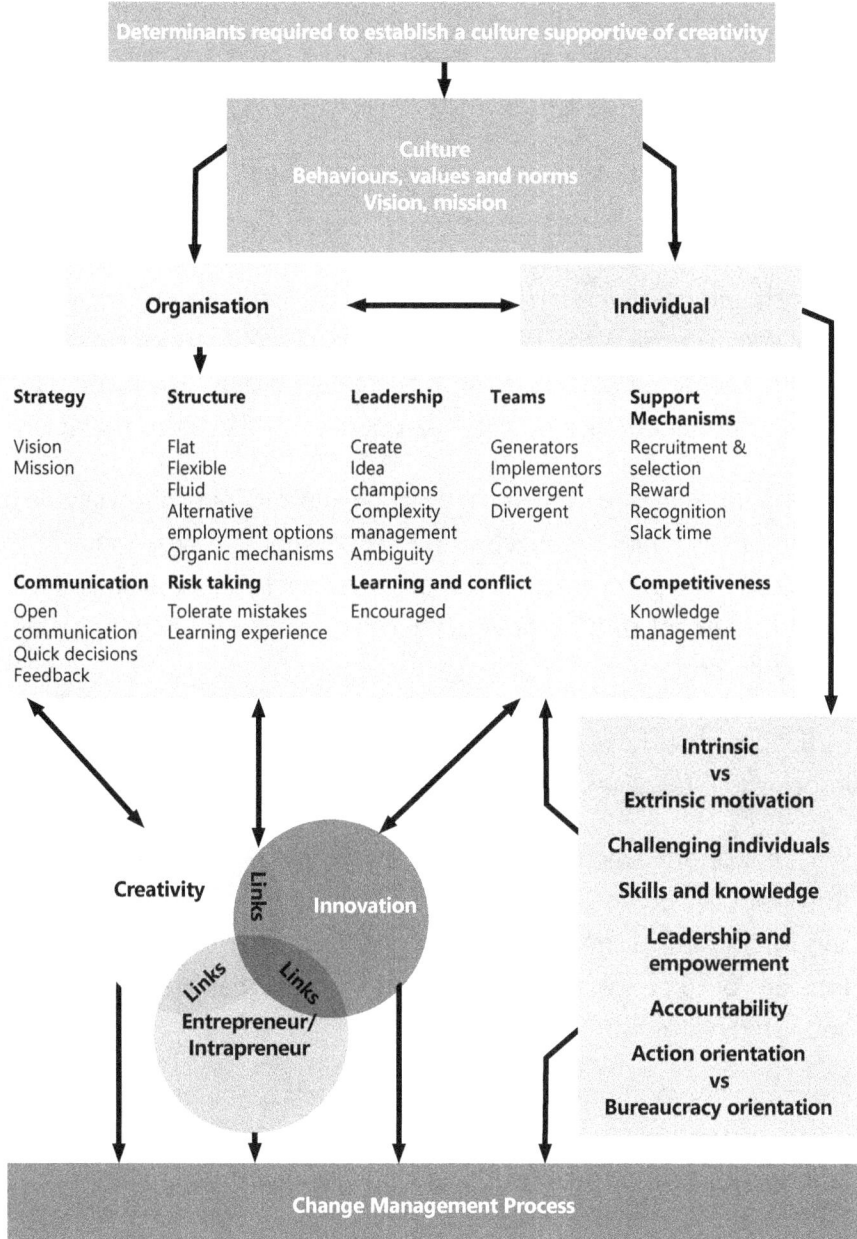

Figure 2: Determinants required to establish a culture supportive of creativity

A high-level overview of some of the determinants will be discussed. Organisations should ideally design a strategy that is able to convert creative potential into commercial application. Organisations have to design a strategy to mine and/or develop the latent CQ of the employees to enable them to apply the CQ in order to design solutions of how to navigate the challenges posed by the 4IR. Creativity in organisations and the willingness to apply the latent or acquired CQ is dependent on an appropriate context.

Creative organisations have strategies that are built on a flexible but firm context, which includes some or all off the following elements, e.g. culture, leadership style, values, structures, systems, skills and resources. The latter elements should be aligned in a way to form the necessary synergy to foster creativity and to enable the latent and acquired CQ to effectively play and be applied in organisations. Structures of creative organisations are flat, fluid, flexible, allow for alternative employment options and evolve organically.

An organisational culture that promotes creativity and innovation should allow employees time to think creatively and to experiment. In organisations where creativity and innovation are encouraged, personnel are, for example, allowed to spend 15 percent of their time on generating new ideas and working on their favourite projects.

Jeffrey Baumgartner has some ideas on how to create a more creative office. He proposes the following ten steps: (Adapted with permission.)[13]

1. Most important: Deep down in your corporate heart of hearts, you must truly want to become a creative company. Ask yourself: do you want your shop-floor staff pestering you with their notions of how to improve the firm or your secretary demonstrating that she has cleverer ideas than you? Think about it.

2. Encourage humour in your office. If your staff members feel they cannot laugh, they probably cannot be creative either. If your office is devoid of laughter, there are two things you can do to encourage humour:

3. Laugh at jokes. If you are not used to laughing, practise in front of the mirror. Bad laughing can be frightening.

4. Allow staff to e-mail each other jokes. A good way of doing this is by e-mailing your staff occasional jokes. If you do not know any jokes you are probably working too hard. A word of caution – keep it professional.

5. Build creative teams, with highly creative people as leaders. Empowering each individual employee to be a creative genius is not practical. Indeed, many staff members are quite happy doing their work as they always have done. Forcing them to be creative on their own will only increase the angst. But, once they are part of a creative team with a creative leader, they will loosen up.

6. Creative teams should comprise people from a wide range of disciplines and backgrounds. If you are trying to invent a better wheel, don't just put wheel specialists on the creative team. Include farmers, grandmothers, philosophy students, butchers, bakers and candlestick makers. Or whoever. The important thing is to get the widest range of disciplines possible. However, the team leader should be a naturally creative person who inspires others (hopefully you have a few such souls on your payroll).

7. Brainstorm problems regularly – and with a multidisciplinary creative team (if you don't know what this is, you haven't read the previous item!) Refer to the section on THE STEP-BY-STEP GUIDE TO BRAINSTORMING!

8. Even if you are not an advertising agency, hire a creative director to promote creativity and be creative. She/he should be the kind of person who not only bubbles over with creative ideas, but who also encourages others to be creative. She/he should also be involved in all departments of the company.

9. Establish a means of publishing, sharing and storing ideas. This can be as simple as a bulletin board where people can pin ideas or as complex as an Intranet-based idea bank. Alternatively, designate a long white wall as an idea graffiti zone, leave markers near the wall and invite staff to write their ideas on the wall in bright colours.

10. Ensure that people who dare to have and announce ideas are rewarded. Telling staff their ideas are stupid (even if they are stupid) also tells staff you don't want to hear about new ideas. Likewise, ignoring ideas and hoping they go away will work only too well. Soon, staff will not bother you with their ideas. Rather, listen to all new ideas, think them over for at least a day, reward the staff for suggesting the idea and, if it is not doable, explain why. Then invite the staff to think about alternative solutions.

i. Give staff the opportunity to go for walks, stare out the window, lie down on the sofa, perform meditation on the floor, or whatever helps their brainwaves flow. Different people have different ways of thinking. Most people, however, are at their creative worst sitting behind a desk with a stack of papers on the left and a computer on the right.

ii. Be aware that creativity is a long-term investment and it will not bring an immediate return. If your company is not creative now, it will take time for management and staff to adopt new ways of thinking, behaving and producing. Then, once ideas start flowing, they must be implemented. This also takes time. But, over the long term, the payoff can be very big indeed. So, don't just sit there, go for it! Or, use Virgin's motto – "Screw it, let's do it!"

King Price Insurance and Missing Link, a presentation training company, are two South African organisations where the environments are prime examples of a physical office space aimed at supporting creativity and innovation.

King Price Office Environment supporting Creativity and Innovation

Chapter 2: Determinants Required to Create a Culture Supportive of Creativity

Missing Link Office Environment supporting Creativity and Innovation

Missing Link Office Environment supporting Creativity and Innovation

Leaders must generate and create the right environment for creativity and innovation. They should focus the best efforts of talented individuals to build innovative successful groups and teams. Lize Wiseman[14] coined the term "multipliers" and lists the following secrets of leaders who are multipliers:

- They attract the right talent

- They retain the best, most creative people and help them to achieve their best potential

- They find a larger than life challenge

- They ignite debates and encourage different views to be expressed

Humane leadership must be the 4IR's real innovation. The CEO-to-worker pay ratio is still a bone of contention. Deaths related to stress, toxic workplaces and bad management are on the rise. Organisations, institutions and societies are going through a major crisis. Performance continues to decline whether measured through return on assets or return on invested capital despite rising labour productivity. The average life expectancy of Fortune 500 companies has decreased from 75 to 15 years in the past 50 years. Data shows that only 13% of the workforce is passionate about their work despite the resources spent on learning and development (L&D). Global figures show 80% of employees are less than fully engaged at work. The old leadership model doesn't work anymore. A big shift in leadership and management is required.[15]

The first step is to start with individual leaders and determine their beliefs, goals, ways of handling people and their understanding of strategy. They need to start to perceive their organisation as a dynamic entity and not an inert set of assets. Leaders need to possess some degree of Emotional Intelligence. They need to have a good idea of their weaknesses and strengths. They need to be in possession of information of how all the business units are operating. Coaching is a very efficient tool with which to increase self-awareness and reduce blind spots of leaders and managers. The management shift needed to adapt to the 4IR is divided into two categories: individual and organisational.

For the individual shift, senior leaders and managers need to fully understand their teams and learn how to impact them. Research supports the concept of Levels of engagement and performance from Level 1, which is apathetic, through to level 5, which is passionate and unbounded. This emergent leadership model draws on social neuroscience and complexity theory, as well as empirical research on employee engagement and organisational behaviour.

Each level is characterised by distinct mindsets and behaviours. With coaching and facilitated discussion, people can improve. A significant change occurs when moving from Level 3 to Level 4. This is the key moment of the management shift: the point at which high performance begins. Level 4 is the level at which leadership 4.0 emerges. This level of leadership is needed for surviving and thriving in the 4IR.

The phases that the leader must go through are:

- **Level 1:** Lifeless/Apathetic – "I am demoralised – there is nothing I can do to change the situation".

- **Level 2:** Reluctant/Stagnating – "I am frustrated – there is no point in trying too hard".

- **Level 3:** Controlled/Orderly – "I need to be in control – I am reluctant to share information".

- **Level 4:** Enthusiastic/Collaborative – "We can achieve great things as a team – I respect myself and others".

- **Level 5:** Unlimited/Unbounded – "I inspire others to achieve their unlimited potential – I am living a fulfilled life".

The idea is to ultimately transform a more authoritarian leadership style into a more participative style. This usually inspires a more people-focused culture. A comprehensive approach to the development of leaders, their teams and the wider organisation can have a dramatically positive effect. The effect of empowered teams permeates to the rest of the organisation. The enthusiasm and energy ignite underperforming teams to at the very least, try harder.

In conclusion: the 4IR has a disruptive effect on leadership. Organisations where leadership is based on fear and control no longer work. A new leadership model is needed, a model where leadership understands what is happening across the company and where the leader is empowered to lead the organisation in line with a defined moral code guided by ethical choices and responsibilities. A true shift towards **humane leadership,** where trust and respect permeate organisations, is required in an era where routine and mundane tasks are going to be performed by machines and where the human element is going to become more important than ever.[16]

Steve Jobs[17], on the other hand, convinced people that they can do the impossible and then he magically enabled them to do it and carry it off. Current leaders need to enhance the CQ of future leaders by creating an environment supportive of creativity and innovation. It is crucial that the right **teams** are assembled when organisations want to optimally mine and apply the latent CQ of the individual team members. A creative team, whether it's musicians, theatre troops or business teams require trust, familiarity of members with each other, collaboration and a shared commitment to the same goals to optimally unleash their Creative Intelligence. Cognitive psychology and neuroscience have taught us that we all possess the ability to be creative and a more socio-cultural approach offers insights as to how we must act in a social context to be creative. The questions to then be explored are: how does creativity emerge from collaboration and how does it thrive in a social context? In an era of huge social change and the explosion of social media the question remains: What must leaders and managers do to create an environment supportive of creativity?

Leaders and managers need to turn the team experience into an adventure. They need to utilise methodologies, frameworks, techniques and tools to first unlock the individual creative potential. They need to enable individuals to believe in their abilities to create and that their **CQ can be improved by collaborating with the right people.** They then need to extend the ideas generated in a team set-up to achieve innovation at scale. Innovation is, after all, creativity commercialised. If organisations want teams to innovate routinely then they need to nurture an innovation culture. One of the current trends is customer-focused innovation. Organisations need to find the best way to leverage creative resources in support of organisational goals. Creatively confident organisations and teams are not built overnight.

Working through the change curve and **developing the creative confidence** of individuals in teams should ideally occur in tandem. A lot of individuals resist embarking on a creative quest and state that they are not creative. This can be viewed as part of the avoidance/denial stage in the change process. Some individuals in teams may display hidden signs of rejection. This can correlate with the anger stage in the change process. Team members progress to the acceptance stage once they are trained on how to use the methodologies, frameworks, techniques and tools to boost their creative confidence. They then dare to take a leap of faith by taking action. Their ideas are then implemented. The results are then verified and evaluated. Feedback should be given, and improvements made should any be required.

The following requirements and determinants should also be taken into consideration when working with teams. It is important to make sure that some members of the team have domain-relevant skills. Prior knowledge should be assessed. Knowledge gaps should be addressed. Establishing a culture supportive of creativity and innovation takes time and it can be a step-by-step approach in some cases. **Teams and organisations must realise that technology is not enough anymore – people need to acquire technical business skills and soft skills as well.** To enable individuals and teams to unleash their latent creative potential and to share their ideas, support from both the top and the bottom (troops in the trenches as well as the generals) is required. People at every level need to understand how to inflame the **culture** and cultivate **change.**

Encourage people to keep at it – it is like a toddler learning to walk, a young child learning how to ride a bicycle or a young adult trying to drive a car. All these activities require lots of practice, repetition and encouragement. The same is the case with creativity. Keep your sense of humour and build on the energy of others. Minimise hierarchy and value team commitment and trust. Defer judgement at least temporarily. Boost the confidence of the team members by being open to whatever they share, verbally or visually. It does not have to be perfect. It does not have to make sense at the time.

At some stage a shift from individual creativity and innovation to team ownership is required. The multidisciplinary and diverse teams need to collaborate by optimally utilising everyone's varied experiences and controversial perspectives. This will assist teams to be able to present and implement their creative and innovative ideas in a VUCA (volatile, uncertain, complex and ambiguous) world filled with multi-dimensional challenges.

There will always be sceptics, cynics and prophets of doom and gloom in every team. They resist change and may be limited by one or a few creative blocks. The confidence in their creative abilities may have been tarnished. Their initial creative offerings may have been so severely critiqued that their inner Da Vinci, Einstein and Picasso require some serious triggers for them to access and unleash their creativity again. Warren Bennis[18] states that great groups/teams believe they can do what no one else can do or have done before. They have plans of actions – their goals are "dreams with deadlines". Highly creative teams take ownership of their results.

Support mechanisms such as recruitment and selection strategies, reward and recognition and slack-time are determinants that can also be effectively utilised to create an environment supportive of creativity and innovation. Recruiting and appointing people from diverse backgrounds should lead to richer ideas and processes that should stimulate creativity and innovation. If creative behaviour and innovation are rewarded it will become the general dominant way of behaviour. Many organisations hope that people will think more creatively and take risks but reward them for well-proven, trusted methods and fault-free work. Creating time and space in people's lives for reflection, ideation and experimentation are likely to result in establishing critical preconditions for making breakthroughs happen.

Open and transparent communication based on trust, the way in which mistakes are handled and the comfort of employees that know the level of risk that they can safely take also promote a culture supportive of creativity and innovation. Understanding different thinking styles and training employees in the process of constructive confrontation will create a culture supportive of creativity and innovation. The most creative and innovative departments in an organisation regard competitiveness as an important part of their culture.

They spot trends and act on them expeditiously.

A high-level overview of the organisational determinants required to establish an environment supportive of creativity and innovation was provided. The focus will now shift to the individual determinants required for creativity and innovation. Intrinsic motivation is a key driver of creativity. Extrinsic motivation like money may ignite creativity and innovation temporarily. It can also inhibit creativity and innovation since certain terms and conditions must be adhered to, to be eligible for the monetary incentive. Open-ended and non-structured tasks engender higher creativity than narrow jobs by people responding positively when they are challenged and provided with ample scope to generate novel solutions. Domain-relevant skills such as expertise, technical skills and talent can have positive as well as negative consequences. On a positive level, knowledge enhances the possibility of creating new understanding. On a negative level, high domain-relevant skills may narrow the search heuristics to learnt routines and thereby constrain new perspectives. The ideal might be the training of a multitude of employees and providing them with methodologies, frameworks, techniques and tools while encouraging them to apply these tools to foster a culture supportive of creativity and innovation.

Empowering people to innovate is one of the most effective ways for leaders to mobilise the energies of people to be creative. Combined with leadership support and commitment, empowerment gives people freedom to assume responsibility for innovation. Empowerment in the presence of strong cultures that guide actions and behaviour produces both energy and enthusiasm for consistent work towards an innovative goal. Employees themselves can devise ways that allow them to innovate and accomplish their tasks. One of the problems with empowerment occurs when it is provided in an organisation without a strong value system capable of driving activities in a unified and aligned manner to the super-ordinate goals of the organisation. In these conditions, empowerment is little less than abdication of responsibility and when responsibility and power are pushed downwards, chaos typically ensues.

Even with empowerment, innovative actions can be incapacitated. Often people encounter organisational barriers that inhibit innovation. Some typical organisational barriers encountered are self-imposed barriers, unwarranted assumptions, one-correct-answer thinking, failing to challenge the obvious, pressure to conform and the fear of looking foolish. Leaders should first put mechanisms in place and design interventions to address these organisational barriers that inhibit creativity and innovation.

Leadership actions should ensure that there is a fine balance between empowerment and guidance. Responsibility and power still reside with the leader. It should be properly clarified who is accountable for which deliverables.

A very common problem in empowered innovation is that everyone is encouraged to participate in cross-functional process involvement, often to an extent that almost everybody loses track of who is accountable for what. The result of unrestricted and uncontrolled empowerment is chaos. Some advocate "chaos within guidelines" while others propose "freedom within a framework". As new processes are put in place, new forms of behavioural guidance should be provided and accompanied by redefinitions of responsibility. While on the surface, empowerment resembles an unstructured process, it is anything but that. Empowerment is in fact a clear definition of 1) domains in which the individuals can exert creative discretion, and 2) the responsibility that individuals have to bear while engaging in their total task as employees of the organisation.

Krippendorff[19] proposes that the innovation should be congruent with or replace three levels of accountability:

- Individual: promises made should be kept.

- Organisation: commitments people make when they choose to join the organisation; innovations that conflict with any of these are unlikely to be embraced.

- Societal: organisations and individuals operate in a network of social accountabilities that we have implicitly accepted by belonging to our communities.

For innovation to stick, you have to eventually change, or fit in with the web of accountabilities that hold together your organisation, partners and users.

To ensure that innovation occurs, leaders must ascertain that no bureaucratic bottlenecks suffocate attempts at innovation. One such primary culprit is overly bureaucratic procedures for rubber-stamping approval or reporting requirements. Faced with obstacles such as these, many employee initiatives fail. In fact, a large proportion of suggestion schemes appear to fail, not due to a lack of ideas but because of the protocols, and the failure of the protocols to process with sufficient speed either a favourable or unfavourable response. Employee innovativeness is not always the stumbling block – often the organisational processes and structures are so burdensome and unwieldy that they create a high level of unresponsiveness. Leadership commitment to re-engineer out unfruitful elements of bureaucracy processes and structure can lay the foundation for a climate of innovation.

The above section discussed some of the determinants required on an organisational as well as on an individual level that are required to establish an environment supportive of creativity and innovation. Creating a culture supportive of creativity and innovation is a complex and long-term endeavour and a kaleidoscope of determinants can be employed.

Language is another determinant to be employed and a powerful tool with which to establish and shape a culture supportive of creativity and innovation. To change attitudes and behaviour, change the vernacular. Influence the dialogue about new ideas and you will influence broader patterns of behaviour. Do not underestimate the power of positive vocabulary. Creatives, designers and innovators need a new vocabulary and a new repertoire of methodologies. Terms like 'ideas', 'breakthroughs', 'user focus', 'visualisation', 'failing fast', CX (Customer Experience), UX (User Experience), DX (Digital Experience) and TX (Transformational Experience) were attempts to understand and implement Design Thinking and innovation. Powerful terminology intends to shift behaviour and should ideally evolve in tandem with our efforts to shape and make sense of a world that is in the process of being created. A side note: write manuals and instructions in the language of the typical consumer and not in the language of the engineers or technical experts who designed them.

Culture is a collection of deeply held attitudes, entrenched habits, repeated behaviours, latent emotions and collective perceptions of the world. Culture is the shared set of assumptions we all bring when we work together – our unspoken expectations of one another. The fact that culture determines an organisation's success is an idea whose time has come. You need cultural insight before you can take cultural action. Culture is mostly defined as "the way we do things around here". It takes patience, perseverance and a personality larger than life to establish a culture supportive of creativity and innovation. It takes a long time to embed and spread a culture supportive of creativity and innovation. Organisational culture can be inspired by:

- Sharing case studies and success stories: these are more powerful persuaders than metrics and results
- Showing-off the prototypes
- Training across disciplines
- Fostering a "Let's solve it" attitude
- Encouraging creative energy at every level of the organisation
- Mapping the informal creativity networks inside the organisation
- Nurturing and embracing the "creativity outlaws"
- Finding out why people break the rules
- Questioning why the rules existed in the first place

Organisations need to unify their people around a common, clear, cultural intent, driven by a core of identified keystone behaviours and positive emotions. Create a culture supportive of creativity and innovation by focusing on what really matters. An organisation has many traits but only a few are vital symbols of the new culture you are trying to establish. Select the behaviours that need to be adhered to in order to establish a culture supportive of creativity and innovation. Encourage the desired organisational behaviours by asking the right questions such as: "What keeps you from being more innovative?" or "How can we encourage people to experiment more?" and "How do we get people to collaborate more?" A high level of empathy, great persistence and resolve, rigorous focus, and a practical approach needs to be designed in order to mine and unleash the latent CQ residing within the organisation. You need to find and discover the critical few that have already show-cased their CQ or are constantly trying to show-off their CQ. The creative confidence of the critical few needs to be cultivated and their emotional commitment needs to be obtained. **Use your early adopters and explore the pockets in your organisation where CQ@Play is evident.** Celebrate the achievements of your early adopters. Keep on sharing them. Reward creative and innovative ideas.

Some organisations create a special place for innovation to occur while others create and design the entire office to look like one big playpen (Missing Link and King Price). Once the context for creativity is set, creative thinking and the application of CQ can be introduced in a number of ways. Organisations should ideally select some methodologies, frameworks, techniques and tools to develop the CQ of their employees.

It is thus clear that a few options should be taken into consideration when organisations want to develop the CQ of their employees. This now begs the question: What is CQ?

# Reflections

- The right environment is crucial if organisations are serious about unleashing the latent creative potential of their employees
- Leaders and managers are responsible to create and establish the determinants required to foster creativity and innovation
- The first step is to unlock the latent creative potential of individuals and to then create teams where individuals feel free to share their ideas
- A shift in ownership from the individual idea to the team taking ownership for implementation must occur
- Language is a powerful tool to be used to create a positive culture supporting and encouraging creativity and sharing of ideas
- Establishing a culture supportive of creativity takes time, repetition, patience and a constant effort
- Creativity is a very crucial component of Creative Intelligence (CQ)

Chapter 3

Creative Intelligence (CQ)

Why CQ?

In order to be able to navigate the challenges posed by the 4IR, humans must develop their CQ and focus on the attributes that will give us the competitive edge over machines. These attributes, for the time being, are empathy, critical thinking, the ability to generate ideas and **creativity**. Howard Gardner shared the view that every person has a unique blend of intelligences. Creativity relies upon the imagination to assist us to see patterns and similarities between unrelated things through metaphors and analogies. Creativity occurs across our various intelligences, bringing them into synergy. Original thinking is about making these connections. Cognitive success is said to be associated with the ability to create analogies. Gardner lists the following eight distinct intelligences that all humans have in a greater or lesser capacity.[20]

- Linguistic Intelligence is the ability to read, write and communicate with words: Tell stories, write essays, participate in interviews, and converse regularly with peers.

- Logical-Mathematical Intelligence is the ability to reason and calculate, to think things through in a logical, systematic manner: Solve problems, balance chequebooks, create schedules and even budget money.

- Visual-Spatial Intelligence is the ability to think in pictures, visualise a future result and to imagine things in your mind's eye: Paint, draw, design web pages, design rooms, make cards, create logos and draw a couple of mind-maps.

- Musical Intelligence is the ability to make or compose music, to sing well, or understand and appreciate music and the ability to keep rhythm: Attend concerts, play an instrument, hum melodies, sing with others, enjoy rhythms.

- Body-Kinaesthetic Intelligence is the ability to use your body skilfully to solve problems, create products, or present ideas and emotions: Play sports, enjoy movement, walk on tours and notice body language.

- Interpersonal (Social) Intelligence is the ability to work effectively with others, to relate to other people and display empathy and understanding and to notice their motivations and goals: Discuss, exchange ideas and build relationships, work with someone who is totally different to you, share an experience with someone from another culture.

- Intrapersonal Intelligence is the ability for self-analysis and reflection – to be able to quietly contemplate and assess one's accomplishments, to review one's behaviour and innermost feelings, to make plans and set goals, to know oneself: Keep a personal journal, read alone, meditate and study to answer personal questions.

- Naturalistic Intelligence is the ability to recognise fauna and flora, to make other consequential distinctions in the natural world, and to use this ability productively: Collect specimens, garden, follow animal footprints and photograph landscapes. People whose naturalistic intelligence is well developed can be utilised to explore possibilities of biomimicking in the creative process.

> Gardner[21] expanded his research and he has identified another kind of intelligence, namely: Spiritual Intelligence. He defines Spiritual Intelligence as being "a more recent addition to our understanding of our innate intellectual spectrum".

Can you list two examples for each of these intelligences e.g.:

1. Linguistic Intelligence: JK Rowling; Chinua Achebe

2. Musical Intelligence: Lady Gaga; Brenda Fassie

The ideal next step is to now develop your CREATIVE INTELLIGENCE!

The question now is: What is Creative Intelligence (CQ) and why CQ? Creative Intelligence is a term that is difficult to **define** and attempts at defining it are very broad. Creative Intelligence is defined in some articles as the **triarchic theory of intelligence**, the group of skills utilised to produce, generate, find, analyse, imagine, and assume.

Bruce Nussbaum does not offer a definition for CQ and he recalls how the term "Creative Intelligence" was conjured up. Several delegates had a discussion at Stanford during the Future of Design Conference and the idea was to explore beyond the design thinking paradigm. Design Thinking works well enough but many at the conference felt that Design Thinking just didn't assist ideas to scale. They believed that given the times that we live in, scale was critical if design was going to have an impact. Some new terms started to emerge. Design Intelligence and CQ (Creative Intelligence) were some of the terms that emerged. Nussbaum concludes this discussion by stating that in the end all agreed that however you named it, assessing this kind of intelligence was very important.

Assessing this kind of intelligence will require a different and unique set of measurement criteria. Criteria that should take into consideration elements such a context, purpose, methodologies, frameworks, tools and techniques used, and integrated with the display of problem-solving, critical thinking, design elements and perhaps an exhibition and/or a portfolio of evidence of some kind. The jury is still out on this. My view is that somebody has to start somewhere as a point of departure.

CQ is viewed by some as a term grouping together the cognitive and non-cognitive aspects of creative generation like intense interest, motivation and other social influences, or a term that refers more to styles of creative thinking. Concepts about CQ widen and broaden the concept of creativity by placing importance on the conceptual, design and environmental variables on the one hand and on thinking processes, applications or styles, on the other. Rowe[22] outlines four styles of CQ:

- Intuition which is based on past experience to guide action

- Innovation which concentrates on systematic and data-orientated problem-solving

- Imagination which uses visualisation to create opportunities

- Inspiration, which emotionally focuses on the changing of something

Creativity and CQ are thus influenced by both the environment and thinking processes employed. Various situations require CQ: the quest for new ideas, the search for yet unknown opportunities, the development of strategies to exploit such opportunities to either address customer needs or to solve a multitude of problems that face individuals throughout their lives. Currently all the CQ that can be mustered should be utilised to re-imagine, re-invent and re-create an unknown future or end-state.

The concept of creative intelligence constitutes elements of our environment, the factors and variables influencing our perceptions and cognitive thinking processes, a motivational trigger, our prior knowledge, our thinking styles, tools that we can employ to enhance creativity, and the product of the process itself, which will either be accepted or rejected as being something creative. If this then is representative of what CQ is, then by manipulating the environmental parameters, being aware of our emotions and other influences upon our perception and thinking, and by developing new thinking styles through the use of methodologies, frameworks, techniques and tools, we can and are, theoretically able to enhance our creative ability.

Claus Moller[23] used Robert Sternberg's work as point of departure and created a more collaborative framework of how to mine and apply CQ to promote creativity and innovation. Creative Intelligent people:

- Actively seek out role models
- Question assumptions
- Allow mistakes
- Take sensible risks
- Seek out tasks that allow for creativity
- Actively define and redefine problems
- Seek and give rewards for creativity
- Allow time to think creatively
- Tolerate ambiguity
- Understand the obstacles creative people must face and overcome
- Are willing to grow
- Recognise the importance of person–environment fit

Susanna Carman describes CQ as an ability to embrace ambiguity and to engage in a sophisticated, nuanced relationship with complexity. She introduces Design Thinking (DT) as a process that cultivates the three basic principles of CQ which she frames as:[24]

- Humility – always start a project, decision-making process or inquiry from a genuine posture of "I don't know"; "It could be…"
- Empathy – the willingness to stand in the shoes of another, to look as they do at a system which they are a part of. Every perspective, however partial, significantly informs design, whether it is the design of public policy or a public toilet
- Curiosity – placing one's attention on sincere exploration, play and discovery with awareness of, but non-attachment to, personal agenda or expected outcome.

The challenge of 'how do you do it' remains. I was asked by one of my clients in 2018 to use a specific Design Thinking methodology in order to assist a division to design a new Target Operating Model. The client expressed the opinion that this specific Design Thinking methodology can be used even if the team is not creative. A new Target Operating Model was designed but it was a very clinical model based to a large extent on the current model. Incremental improvements were made. There were no disruptive or breakthrough ideas. It was pretty much more of the same. It was a very structured approach and at its best led to some incremental improvements. Some thought leaders, and even the designers of this approach, have since concurred that the very linear approach of some Design Thinking methodologies can stifle creativity and even inhibit breakthrough ideas.

Developing CQ in your organisation requires a culture supportive of creativity and innovation. It requires a mindset where the organisation nurtures and acknowledges the creators and the innovators. Actions and activations should be planned in such a manner that they ignite and encourage creativity and innovation in your organisation. Mine, unleash and liberate the creativity within your workforce. Draw on the latent creative potential of the organisation. Listen to the people. Be mindful of the creative energy displayed in the organisation and tap into that knowledge when it happens.

CQ can be found across many fields and disciplines, in all spheres of life. People who do not perceive themselves to be creative are drawing on many of the same skills as those a musician or writer would use. CQ is social. Creative ability is increased by learning from others, collaborating and sharing. Creativity cannot be done in a vacuum – and even if you could – you cannot afford to. Creative collaboration is key in a time of instability and immense change.

Bruce Nussbaum[25] is of the opinion that CQ comprises of the following competencies: knowledge mining (find out what you don't know you know), framing (understanding your way of seeing the world as it compares with other people's), playing (a superior alternative to problem-solving), making (a making–culture revolution where making things is becoming a critical component of innovation) and pivoting (moving beyond the creative idea in order to create new products and services).

Creativity or CQ must become part of the individual as well as the organisation's DNA. It must become an integral part of how individuals and organisations operate. It is about actively utilising creativity methodologies, frameworks, techniques and tools to solve problems, identify gaps, spot patterns and trends, derive insights and then to actively pursue the commercial implementation of your idea. Use the chosen definition as point of departure to evaluate the creative gift – the product, service or new business model – by assessing performance of specific tasks or reviewing a body of work. Creativity and Creative Intelligence (CQ) cannot be measured by standardised tests or a checklist.

Bruce Nussbaum's book, amply titled *Creative Intelligence*, is currently one of the few books about CQ and I have relied heavily on his findings to write this chapter.[26] I would like to conclude this chapter with my attempt at defining Creative Intelligence. Watch this space!

Creative Intelligence (CQ) is knowing which methodologies, frameworks, techniques, tools and intelligences to use when, how and where to address client needs and to solve problems while imagining, inventing, creating and shaping the future.

Please feel free to create your own definition of Creative Intelligence and be so kind as to share it with me via LinkedIn.

Claus Moller[27] states that Creative Intelligence is the ability to go beyond the existing to create novel and interesting ideas. This description aligns with several definitions used in attempts to define creativity. Creativity and CQ remain terms and concepts that are difficult to define. We need to do more on all levels to encourage and support the development of Creative Intelligence. Creativity is a very important component of Creative Intelligence as formerly stated. Creativity is cited on most of the future skills lists as being one of the top ten skills required to navigate the challenges posed by the 4IR. The next chapter will provide an overview of the future skills, some factors to consider regarding these skills and a more comprehensive view with regard to creativity.

Reflections

- Humans should ideally focus on skills and attributes that machines don't have in order to futureproof their value-add navigating the 4IR
- Creativity is cited as one of the top ten future skills
- Gardner identified 8 intelligences that all humans possess to some degree
- Spiritual Intelligence (SQ) and Creative Intelligence (CQ) have recently been added to the cadre of the esteemed spectrum of intelligences
- CQ is difficult to define and the concept is still evolving organically
- Creativity and CQ operate symbiotically and are dependent on the environment and thinking processes employed
- CQ is required to re-think, re-create, re-invent and re-imagine the future
- CQ can be developed
- Creative intelligent people display certain behaviours
- Creative collaboration is key in a time of instability and immense change
- Opinions are expressed that CQ needs a very specific measuring tool for it to be measured
- Should CQ be measured at all? Measuring is such an archaic concept – the brilliance of CQ@Play should just be recognised, appreciated and enjoyed
- Creative Intelligence is an emerging field still to be explored and developed
- Isn't it time to develop your CQ?

Chapter 4

Future Skills and Creativity

Why is creativity cited to be one of the top ten skills required to enable us to navigate the challenges posed by the 4IR?

The 4IR complicates the challenge of the supply and demand of skills. The rapidly expanding use of robots and process automation, big data to create smarter supply chains and the use of artificial intelligence (AI) for decision-making have helped to redefine the work week, and created a new economy of gig-based independent contractors who are reshaping when and where work is done. For businesses to remain competitive, they should rethink how and where work is done, thereby potentially reshaping their organisational structures, cultures and processes to fit these changing developments. The speed of technological updates often surpasses the speed at which current and future talent can be upskilled and trained, leaving a gap between skills needed and skills available. This blurred the traditional definitions of formal and informal employment. Many jobs will disappear while a new set of jobs will emerge.[28] **Jobs that don't exist currently will be powered into being by creativity.**

An approach consisting of blended methodologies is not an option to be considered but an integral part of the reality of the impact of the 4IR. The design needs to take into consideration the Baby Boomers with their challenges to adapt to the digital world and who do not always keep up with the pace of change. The realities of younger generations that are tech savvy and have already embraced a digital world should be factored in too. The design must align with the predicted future skills and the content must prepare future leaders for the new ways of work.

The transition from classroom learning to online learning remains a challenge. Generations have been subjected to classroom learning and the adoption and up-take of online learning may take some time. The future is now, and the Learning and Development strategies of organisations must embrace an agile and collaborative approach with designs having to take a myriad of factors ranging from what the trends indicate to taking the different generations and socio-economic realities into consideration.

STEM (science, technology, engineering and mathematics) skills are going to be more important than ever but do not forget the SMAC (social, mobile, analytics and cloud) skills. Learning these skills/platforms will make you stand out in the future job market. Interdisciplinary knowledge will also give you the competitive edge in the future job market.[29]

Future careers will require you to pull information from many different fields to come up with creative solutions to future problems. This skill is easy to acquire. Start by reading as much as you can about anything and everything that interests you. It is evident that creativity is featured on all the future skills lists. **But what is CREATIVITY?**

If you are asked to think about at least 4 people you consider to be creative, who do you think about? Did your thoughts conform to the names that most frequently come to mind namely, Leonardo da Vinci, Bach, Beethoven and Mozart? Or did you think more widely and list artists (Van Gogh, Picasso, Sekoto), poets and writers (Shakespeare, Keats, Mashigo, Nyathi, Smith)? You may have listed sculptors (Michelangelo, Khumalo, Villa) and composers (Liszt, Puccini, Hofmeyr, Ibrahim, Masekela). What about scientists like Einstein, Edison, Barnard and Amoils?

Does that mean that creativity is restricted to a handful of artists, musicians, scientists and the like? Do people vary in degrees of creativity? Can you learn to be more creative? Continue reading and decide for yourself ...

Being creative is not just for artists, poets, musicians, or scientists, as previously stated. Everyone has the potential to do things in new ways – ways that make their jobs and their lives more fun and rewarding. Everyone is creative and creativity can be developed, acquired and exercised. Some people, though, can draw on their creativity more easily than others. As a result, they put their talents to greater use and bring a greater enthusiasm and exuberance to their work. The flipside is that creativity may scare some of us.

Everyone has the potential to do things in new ways – ways that make their jobs and their lives more fun and rewarding. Everyone is creative and creativity can be developed, acquired and exercised.

Amabile[30, 31, 32] suggests that creative people possess three types of skills, namely domain-relevant skills (e.g. specific knowledge regarding a discipline), creative-relevant skills (e.g. thinking skills), and task-motivation (e.g. to be motivated). Everybody has the potential to be creative and the characteristics that enhance creativity are present to a greater or lesser extent in every individual. Creative practice functions to integrate intellectual, social, emotional, aesthetic, physical and perceptual elements.

Creativity is sometimes the result of happy accidents such as the discoveries of penicillin and the pacemaker. Sometimes mistakes or mishaps can turn into breakthrough successes. There are numerous such examples where success stemmed from what at first sight appeared to have been a failure. Sometimes creativity stems from a happy accident. Goodyear discovered vulcanisation when he spilled a mixture of rubber and sulphur on the stove. We don't think of ourselves as creative because we don't know how to identify creativity. We don't even know how to define it properly.

Various authors and researchers agree that creativity is difficult to define but some have bravely offered a definition of creativity. For instance, Guilford[33, 34] refers to new inventions and Barron[35, 36] to "the creation of something new". Tannenbaum[37] suggests that creativity is a useful process because it improves communication, promotes learning and the exploration of the problem, and helps to develop new ideas, solutions and/or alternatives.

All the above authors seem to agree that creativity should result in something new.

West and Farr[38] describe creativity as "the creation of something new as a result of the individual's own competence or due to the interaction between the individual and his/her **ENVIRONMENT**. The importance of an environment supportive of creativity and innovation has been discussed earlier in the book.

Organisations are becoming increasingly interested in examining how individuals and organisations can co-create an innovative and creative **CULTURE**. Culture was also discussed earlier in the book. This interest is fuelled by the desire to understand the link between culture and the influence it has on individuals creatively having to develop and initiate new products, services and systems.

Common elements such as the characteristics of the creative person, creative processes and environments that promote creativity and manifestations of creativity are often found in definitions of creativity.

Then there are those who are of the opinion that a creative idea without *commercial application* is irrelevant. If creativity is viewed in an organisational context, the evaluation and application should focus on a commercial outcome. Organisations will not invest to develop creative thinking and problem-solving skills if these are not linked to business outcomes. However, if creativity is linked to business outcomes, the creative result must be evaluated and measured.

Creativity as a context-specific evaluation can vary from one group, one organisation, or one culture to another. Moreover, it can also change over time. Creativity should therefore be evaluated at different levels: at the level of the person and the profession, the organisation and industry in which it operates and where it is intended to produce a tangible result.

Creativity should be measured in context if the outcome of the creative process is intended for commercial purposes. Creativity of employees and teams should be utilised for the generation of new and useful/valuable ideas for products, services, processes and procedures by individuals or groups in a specific organisational context. From the above it is evident that a kaleidoscope of factors has to be considered when attempting to define creativity.

The concept "creativity" in most definitions implies something new. "Developments" implies products, processes, systems, customer service or anything new in an organisational context. "Interaction" refers to any action needed to produce the development. This process, according to the definitions already discussed and other alternative definitions that were explored can either be the result of an individual action or the intended outcome of a group or team. "Environment" refers to the place and circumstances that support the manifestation of creative result. The concept "commercial intent" implies that a business breakthrough (more about breakthroughs later) needs to be the result of the creative attempt/effort and that a return on investment is expected.

As you can see, creativity remains a construct that is difficult to define.

Therefore, creativity needs to be defined in context. It is always advisable to create your own definition of creativity as point of departure! Nothing prevents you from changing it should you be required to do so!

I created the following definition of creativity:

> Creativity is the accomplishment of new developments as a result of the interaction between an individual and his/her environment, or groups and their environment with commercial intent.

This definition of creativity must be viewed in a business and organisational context!

In the business world, creativity manifests itself as innovation.

Creativity is unequivocally one of the most sought-after future skills required to not only survive but to thrive in the 21st century. Are you sufficiently creative to re-imagine, re-create and re-invent the new world that beckons? Take the Creativity Self-Test on the next page to find out for yourself!

Creativity Self-Test

Seriously, you can use this test to determine how creative you are – (adapted from *http://www.innovint.com/downloads* then click on the creativity test.)

> After completing the questionnaire, complete the key to determine your level of creativity. Rate yourself on each statement below from 0-4 (Strongly Disagree - 0, Disagree - 1, Neutral - 2, Agree - 3, or Strongly Agree - 4).

	STATEMENT	CHOICE
1	Creativity is a regular part of how I perform my job (or responsibilities).	
2	I have mastered a set of creativity skills that I use on a regular basis.	
3	I am receptive to ideas that challenge my way of thinking.	
4	Time restraints are not a problem for me in being creative in the workplace.	
5	I regularly take time to learn and implement advanced creativity techniques.	
6	I am receptive to team creativity, even if rewards are shared equally between all team members.	
7	I have an in-depth knowledge of the areas of my job that require me to be creative.	
8	I consistently take my ideas from conception to application.	
9	I am not limited by my position with respect to implementing creative ideas.	
10	I am aware of my unique way of being creative and I use it on a regular basis.	
	TOTAL	
	(Multiply your total by 2.5 to obtain your total creativity quotient based upon 100%)	%

The average score of individuals taking this assessment is 72%.

Key for scores

90% – 100% Extremely Creative

Creativity is a natural part of your life and you have no problem integrating it into your work life. This book will merely confirm what you already know.

80% – 90% Very Creative

You are probably most creative in response to the problems you encounter, rather than it being a skill naturally used in every part of your life. You will benefit from the problem-solving techniques and/or exercises in this book.

70% – 79% Creative

You are creative and know how to implement it. However, there are self-imposed limitations (and probably organisational barriers) that prevent you from routinely using it in problem solving and challenging opportunistic situations. Take a conscious decision to be more creative.

50% – 70% Creatively Challenged

You are probably creative in practice, on occasions. This book will assist you to be more mindful and aware of your latent creative potential.

Below 50% Not Creative at All

You are not creative at all. This book may be just what you need!

It has now been mentioned a couple of times that everyone is creative and that creativity can be developed. You now have a better idea of how creative you are. But how much do you really know about creativity? There are a couple of myths with regard to creativity that exist. There are also a couple of real and/or imagined barriers to creativity. Can you think about things that can threaten or stifle creativity? Do you know what your own perceptions are about your own creativity? Do you stifle and inhibit your own creativity? Continue reading and you may just find the answers you are looking for.

David Burkus[39, 40] lists the following **myths** with regard to creativity:

- **The Eureka Myth:** the notion that all ideas arrive in a "eureka" moment – generating ideas is hard work most of the time.

- **The Breed Myth**: I don't have creative genes – everybody is creative and creativity can be developed.

- **The Originality Myth**: let's assume total credit for a new idea and claim that idea as our own property or the property of our organisation – ideas develop through a much more complicated path, involving more than just one person.

- **The Expert Myth**: the correlation between a person's level of expertise and his or her creative output isn't what you might expect – at a certain level, expertise can actually hinder the creative ability of the individual and decrease their creative output – as expertise grow, creativity sometimes diminishes.

- **The Incentive Myth:** that we commission and reward creative work the same way we do industrial work is part of the incentive myth which is the larger notion that the output and quality of creativity can be increased with incentives.

- **The Lone Creator Myth:** we likewise tend to attribute creative works or innovative ideas to one lone creator, even when that person isn't solely responsible – these stories tend to ignore a truth behind great innovations and creative works: those geniuses typically had teams.

- **The Brainstorming Myth:** when done correctly, brainstorming helps teams assemble a pool of ideas from which they can pick the most novel and useful – but it is rarely done correctly.

- **The Cohesive Myth:** that the most creative ideas and products come from teams that suspend criticism and focus on consensus – an excessive form of cohesiveness, however, can dampen a team's creativity.

- **The Mousetrap Myth:** belief in this myth is built on the assumption that once you have a creative or innovative new product, getting others to see its value is the easy part, and that if you develop a great idea, the world will willingly embrace it – this is often not the case, in fact, it is rarely the case e.g. who wants to hear actors talk?

- **The Constraints Myth:** the myth that creative potential is dampened by constraints when in fact research shows that many innovative teams will tell you that creativity loves constraints – constraints shape our creative pursuits.

There are certain influencers that prevent creativity and creative expression. Perceptual blocks prevent us from clearly perceiving either the problem itself or the information needed to see the problem. Emotional blocks interfere with our freedom to explore and manipulate ideas. Cultural blocks are acquired by exposure to a given set of cultural patterns. Organisational climate or culture can be a barrier or a stimulus to creativity.

Barriers to creativity can also sometimes be reflected and expressed through killer phrases such as "it will never work, it is not practical, it's impossible" and should be avoided.

Below are a few "killer phrases" that you should try to avoid when you hear a new idea. Instead of using one of these the next time you hear a new idea, spend the first 60 seconds thinking about all its possibilities. Even if the idea is finally rejected, you are aware of the idea's rightness and can apply that to another challenge you're facing.

Being critical first, is a costly mistake because it allows excuses to drive the creative thought process. It's amazing to watch a typical new idea interchange. Usually within eight seconds someone proclaims what is wrong with the new idea and then all you see are the pitfalls. Just think if everyone had looked at the pitfalls before they leaped, we'd still be crouched in caves sketching animal pictures on walls.

Figure 3: Killer phrases

The people of *www.whatagreatidea.com* have compiled a list of the top ten "killer phrases":

- It'll never work.
- I don't have time.
- It's not in the budget.
- The boss will never go for it.
- We tried that before.
- That sounds like something my kids would say.
- Let's get a committee to look into this.
- Because I said so.
- Great idea, but not for us.
- It's out of scope.

Consultanese for "We don't get paid to look here."

Write down or think about a couple of "killer phrases" that you have heard before. How did you react to this? What did you learn from this?

Some food for thought: Why were companies that were spending money and time on all the right things failing to come up with the same kinds of life-altering products and services that some twenty-somethings could do with zero budget? Maybe these young ones were not afraid to turn the killer phrases around.

The phrase that will conquer all killer phrases: HOW MIGHT WE…

- How – improvement is always possible
- Might – possibilities
- We – establish ownership

Let's turn all killer phrases into inspirational quotes: What if…

- We don't do what we have always done
- Try what didn't work again
- We try and do it differently
- We rocked the boat
- We can do it without budget
- We can make it fly
- We never use the word "but"

Thinking in Opposites is a very powerful creativity tool!

Fear, particularly fear of failure and fear of change, is one of the biggest blocks to creativity. Most of us fear being criticised or ridiculed, and others are afraid of change, or hold the attitude "if it ain't broke, don't fix it". Black calls these and other blocks of creativity, the G.N.A.T.S of creativity.[41]

As their namesakes, GNATS, imply, G.N.A.T.S. of Creativity are little things that can irritate and cause pain when we least expect it or simply distract us long enough to stop or stifle our creativeness or creative energy.

> "GNATS" is an acronym that stands for Generally Natural Actions (Activities or Attitudes) that Threaten and Stop or Stifle Creativity. Because each of us is susceptible to varying GNATS, Black[42] has developed a list of 26 of them, each starting with a different letter of the alphabet.

They may be caused by ourselves, by people who work with us, by people who we work for, by our clients, by total strangers. They can be real or imagined, true or simply believed to be true, either by ourselves or by those we deal with.

First let's look over a basic list of GNATS. Then the reader can explore how they can be prevented or dealt with when they come "buzzing" around our heads, externally or internally.

AGE	Fearing that you are too young, too old, not young or old enough or were not born in the right age (too soon or too late).
BACKGROUND	You don't have the background to work on the problem or to generate ideas for the topic area.
CULTURE	You live in the wrong culture, a dull culture, or you are not cultured enough to be creative.
DULL	You are feeling dull or are in a dull environment.
EDUCATION	You don't have enough or the wrong education to be creative (no degrees, too many degrees, wrong degree-right school or wrong school).
FOOLISH	You are too foolish to be creative or not foolish enough.
GAMBLE	People see your ideas as too much of a gamble before you work out the pitfalls and turn them into viable solutions and workable plans.
HARD WORK	You don't want to accept that creative problem solving is hard work or that you don't want to work hard enough.

INTELLIGENCE	Creative thinking requires more or less intelligence than you possess.
JEALOUSY	You are always jealous of creative people or you fear others will be jealous of you if you are creative.
KILLED	Your ideas are always being killed by others.
LAUGHTER	Other people just laugh at you when you are creative and they never take you seriously.
MONEY	You don't have the money to be creative or you have too much money and don't need to be creative.
NARROW	Others are too narrow-minded to accept your creative ideas.
OPPORTUNITIES	You never have any great opportunities. Your location, profession, age, etc. can limit these.
PARADIGMS	Yours, mine and ours always get in the way of creativeness.
QUITTERS	You are surrounded by people who quit trying too soon, once they have a workable, acceptable solution they stop trying.
RADICAL	Your ideas are constantly being called "too radical" and because you prefer to be creative most of the time you are labelled as a "radical".
STRESS	You are under too much stress to be creative.
TIME	You don't have the time to spend on being creative you must get your work done now.
UNAPPRECIATED	You always feel unappreciated therefore you have quit trying to be creative for others.
VULTURES	You are surrounded by "vultures", people who steal your ideas and take credit for your ideas as theirs.
WISECRACKS	People respond to your creative ideas with wisecracks, put-downs and put-offs.
XEROGRAPHIC	People are always copying your ideas without giving you credit (similar to "vultures").

	YIELD	You stop or yield to others' criticisms too easily and too often.
	ZIPPED OUT	You have no energy to be creative.

List some of the various GNATS of your Creativity, whether on this list or your own that bother you and develop strategies and strengths to ward them off.

People can inhibit their own creativity by making statements similar to the following:

- "I'm just not a creative person."
- "I never have any good ideas."
- "I don't have time to be creative."
- "I don't know where to get creative ideas."
- "I don't know how people come up with all their creative ideas."
- "I am not arty enough."

According to Perkins[43, 44] creativity does not readily emerge outside of a suitable "climate". His model therefore illustrates the difference between "climate-creating" factors and creative ability. He proposes that a suitable climate includes six basic qualities, which are not demonstrated by all creative people or all forms of creativity in equal measure.

A strong focus on personal aesthetic

This refers to an urge to find order, simplicity and meaning in a chaotic mass of information and impressions, and then to express it. It corresponds to Otto Spranger's[45] view regarding the aesthetic value orientation (being oriented to beauty and the symmetry and harmony of things and events). As part of this, creative people display high tolerance of complexity, ambivalence, disorganisation and asymmetry.

An exceptional ability to spot or discover problems

According to Perkins, creative people devote more time to their personal "agenda of ideas" and think about ideas more than do other people, seeking to verbalise the associated problems. This gives them a range of alternative approaches to problems and enables them to distinguish between pseudo solutions and those that have real potential.

Psychic mobility

Creative people can shift their attention to things that may yield new angles and approaches. An example would be using analogies, like imagining that you are in a similar situation and at a loss for an idea or solution.

A willingness to take risks

Creative people have an extraordinary ability to accept uncertainty and the possibility of failure (the chance that things will not work out as planned). This includes the ability and drive to persist irrespective of failure. Fear of failure, as you will see shortly, is one of the factors that block creativity.

Objectivity

Creative people are not, as popularly believed, victims of their subjective involvement with their creative process and products. Although they are certainly very involved with their talent, they don't live in a private world of creativity. They are characterised by objectivity as they actively seek feedback and advice from experts in their field in order to critically evaluate the merits of their work.

Intrinsic Motivation

The production of a creative work in itself is an end to creative people. Secondary to this is the possibility of material reward, recognition, accolades, and the like. Part of the intrinsic motivation is the challenge, satisfaction and pleasure of producing something that is your own creative work. Research claims that, although creative work often earns considerable rewards, in the long run extrinsic motivation stifles creativity.

The next figure attempts to portray the determinants required to design an intervention aiming to establish an environment supportive of creative thinking and application of CQ on a macro level. Not necessarily all the determinants have to be in place for the successful implementation of a creative intervention in an organisation. The amount of determinants present will determine what should be incorporated into the intervention design to ensure its successful implementation. The determinants can influence the intervention on an independent or interdependent level. The figure should be viewed as an interchangeable vortex.[46]

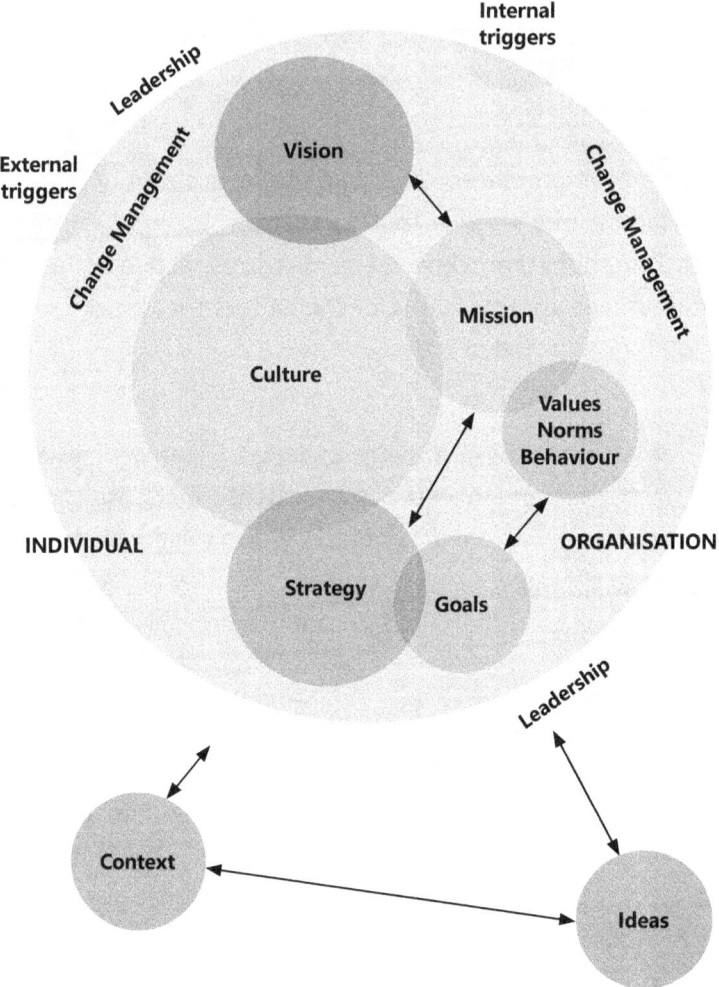

Figure 4: Integrated view of the determinants required to design an innovation intervention on a macro level

How then can organisations enhance the CQ of its members? A possible solution is to develop the creative thinking and problem-solving skills of employees by providing them with selected content and/or workshops that contain methodologies, frameworks, techniques and tools as to how to acquire these skills as well as utilising these skills to enhance and apply their CQ.

No discussion with regard to creativity is complete if the emerging field of **neuroscience** is not mentioned. Some thoughts with regard to neuroscience and creativity are shared. Neuroscience is much more than what is expressed in this section. This is merely my selection of views of what I deemed to be relevant to this book. The views were selected from the following authors: Nussbaum, Betsy & Ong, Leighton and Solikan & Farid.[47, 48, 49, 50]

Neuroscience research has focused, amongst other things, on trying to better understand how the brain enables creative thinking, generates insights, cracks jokes, composes music, solves difficult problems, visualises the image to be conveyed on a canvas, formulates interesting research questions, writes poetry amongst others. A diverse body of research literature ranging from education, cognitive psychology, artificial intelligence, archaeology and cognitive neuroscience indicates that analogy-making is the key underpinning process of intelligence. Importantly, this is not analogy-making in the strict sense often used in intelligence testing, e.g. black is to white as night is to...? Rather, creative thinking requires fluid analogising, where fluid analogies are divergent possibilities@play and the premise that there is more than one correct answer is a given. The constant exploration of possibilities, the endless quest for What if...

The ability to create fluid analogies to explain and clarify concepts and the ability to combine different elements and create a new concept are revered. The ability to employ language that paints pictures is a powerful tool to ignite the imagination. Language is also a very powerful tool to be utilised when introducing change when the end-state is uncertain and needs to be defined and created as the process unfolds. Creative intelligence requires neural systems which are distributed throughout the brain rather than being restricted to specific locations in the brain. Theories with regard to left- and right-brain dominance are still being debated. Machine scanning of the brain has indicated that the entire brain is active when people engage in creative thought.

Conventional IQ tests might not test and/or measure a person's ability to combine different elements to create new concepts which is a crucial component of creative thinking. IQ tests, although indicative of academic success to a certain degree, do not reveal all there is about a person's cognitive potential. Some researchers believe that the pedagogic route to enhancing creative intelligence lies in fluid analogical thinking, and in an ideal classroom, students would be motivated to explore how any concept or piece of knowledge is like another and what insights these possible analogical relationships might afford. The traditional approach to teaching and learning, facts shared, and facts tested, is unfortunately still prevalent in most classrooms.

Creativity requires knowledge, the internalised knowledge that we don't know we know. One must get in touch with the unconscious in order to become more creative. The unconscious ignites the ability to play, to enjoy, to fantasise, to laugh, to loaf and to be spontaneous. Creative playfulness is commonly curbed by trying to conform to fitting into what protocol dictates and creative energy is usually compromised in the process. We lose the ability to play and in the process the gift to explore and ignite the imagination.

Creativity is ignited when a problem needs to be solved. The priority is now to solve the problem. Start by defining the problem and to mentally structure it. This creates both the potential to solve it and inspires original thinking. Utilise methodologies, frameworks, techniques and tools to channel your thinking processes for enhancing creative thought. Tools assist us to look at situations and problems in different ways so we can see new associations and linkages which may lead to new ideas or solutions to problems. One of the most important aspects of seeing new associations and finding solutions to problems is to allow for a period of incubation in order to enable the brain to re-organise information. This is discussed in more detail in the chapter discussing the creative process.

Current views and conversations reflect the hope that science, in particular neuroscience, would be able to explain in the foreseeable future why certain people are more creative than others and we hope that brain scan technology might offer insights about what the rest of us can do to become more creative. Research has indicated that new experiences form new neural pathways. Neural pathways activate the entire brain over time. This forms the rationale for more mature adults to pursue hobbies and activities that are neurologically beneficial.

Advances in brain scan technology might offer insights about what the rest of us can do to become more creative. Powerful machines that generate three-dimensional images of the brain at work were developed and the new field of cognitive neuroscience was born. It is a popular research methodology for analysing creativity. Cognitive neuroscience research has helped demolish several major myths about creativity. Brain scans have shown that creativity is not localised to the right side of the brain. The popular perception was that creativity was generated on the right side of the brain. Creative behaviours activate the entire brain over a period so creativity cannot be reduced to a single flash of insight in a single moment. Creativity is so much more than that single moment and it is much more the individual experiencing that moment.

Neuroscience is not yet able to stimulate part of the brain and causes humans to behave creatively and until that is achieved the best way to understand CQ is to study and learn from the people and organisations who've cultivated it. There are still a lot of gaps in the understanding of neuroscience and Creative Intelligence. Hopefully further advances in technology will enable us to learn and discover more about the connection between neuroscience and CQ as new techniques and information become available. Where does creativity and CQ originate? Does it all start with an idea?

 # Reflections

- The 4IR complicates the challenge of supply and demand of skills

- The workforce of tomorrow must be developed today, and the current workforce must be prepared with an approach that is still to be developed

- The 4IR requires a much more creative and innovative approach than that of Learning and Development

- The design of learning and action learning strategies must include a blended approach combining online elements and content that can be changed frequently with retention-boosting techniques

- Creativity is cited to be one of the top ten skills required to navigate the challenges of the 4IR

- Creativity needs to be defined in context for it to be measured

- Creativity can be the result of hard work, breakthrough ideas or can occur accidentally

- There are a couple of myths with regard to creativity

- Killer Phrases destroy or inhibit creativity – turn them into positive energy by thinking in opposites

- There are real and perceived barriers to creativity – identify your own barriers and find strategies of how to address them

- Certain determinants need to be in place in order to establish a culture supportive of creativity and innovation

- Neuroscience research has focused on trying to better understand how the brain enables creative thinking

- The ability to combine different elements and create a new concept is revered

- Language is a powerful tool to ignite the imagination and orchestrate change

- Machine scanning has shown that the entire brain is active when people engage in creative thought

- The unconscious ignites the ability to play and play in turn ignites the imagination

- The brain needs an incubation period to re-organise information

- Creativity tools assist people to look at situations and problems in different ways so we can see new associations and linkages which may lead to new ideas or solutions to problems

- Current views and conversations reflect the hope that science, and in particular neuroscience, will be able to explain in the forseeable future why certain people are more creative than others

- It all starts with an idea…

The man with a new idea is a crank – until the idea succeeds.

Mark Twain

Chapter 5

Ideas...

Where do ideas come from?

Where does one find inspiration for ideas? How do they originate? Do people who are known for their ideas have a special gift? Or are ideas the result of deliberate and hard work?

Literally, the word "inspiration" means to "breathe into", thus implying that creative ideas come to people via some unexplained divine power. Plato therefore believed that poets were merely interpreters of ideas "breathed into" them by the gods.

> Currently it is acknowledged that "inspiration" (in the sense of a spontaneous experience of an idea that can have a creative outcome) has a lot to do with the way the brain receives and processes information about the things that are high on the "idea agenda" of the creative person.

In terms of the phases of creativity, inspiration seems to take place somewhere between incubation and illumination. Remarkably, it often happens when you are in a state of reduced consciousness, when there is an incoherent, free flow of thought which is not directed to any specific task or problem. That is why you often get your best ideas just before you fall asleep.

Although many writers, painters, composers and scientists will tell you that their creative ideas come out of the blue, it requires a lot of hard analytic work to transform the creative idea into a creative product.

Creativity is 1% inspiration and 99% perspiration![51]

It is all about the idea and to be an innovative company, an organisation should generate a rich portfolio of varied and unusual ideas to encourage the organisational mindset and to instil the desire to put such ideas into action; building a risk-tolerant trust in individuals, even when their ideas are opposing the market trends. Idea generation is a crucial part of the problem-solving process and creativity is the thinking process that helps generate these ideas. If creativity can be improved, then more alternatives, novel approaches or unique solutions are likely to emerge in response to a problem.

It is relatively easy to produce ideas. However, to produce good ideas proves to be more difficult. The challenge is to put these ideas into practice and to commercialise them. Herein lies the main difference between creativity and innovation. Creativity without innovation is without purpose, and innovation without creativity is sterile.

Organisations should build "idea factories" to foster creativity and innovation. Managing the creative and innovative types is a skill to be acquired. Creatives are perceived to be headstrong and to passionately believe in their ideas. Company cultures and managers should nurture such people and find ways in which to mine the ideas of these types and profiles to their advantage. Thinking should ideally be done outside the office. Market the new idea in as many places as possible. Fly under the radar if you must. Run small pilot projects. Share and celebrate quick wins. Most organisations have more ideas than they know what to do with. The main challenge is to know the areas in which to generate the ideas and how to get them implemented. Develop frameworks for further exploration of idea management processes.

Concepts are the building blocks of ideas followed by structure and process. The concept needs to be observed, considered, assembled, prototyped and tested. New ideas are inspired by prior knowledge, a high level of curiosity and intellectual strength. Divergers imagine and convergers do. When you battle to generate ideas, doing the following might inspire: cutting the grass, listening to a church sermon, waking up in the middle of the night, exercising, reading during a boring meeting, falling asleep or waking up, driving, taking a bath or a shower, walking and dancing. Other **Idea Triggers** include changing the physical space you are in, trying something new, trying different things (meals, clothes, magazines, routes to work), creating an idea wall and changing what is on the wall opposite to it, talking to customers inside and outside of your intended target market and adding a touch of target-market and context-appropriate humour.

It is known that diversity triggers a kaleidoscope of ideas. Explore different options, cities and embrace different experiences. Commit to lifelong learning. Integrate elements of creativity, innovation and design thinking. Start a daily journal and begin to take notes. Form a habit, break a habit. Commit to trying at least one creativity technique a day. Repeat something at least 21 times. Prototype, video, sketch – make your idea visual. Implement some ideas and celebrate quick wins – that should lead to more ideas.

There are many ways and places where ideas can be triggered and where inspiration can be sought. There are just as many barriers to ideas and the following **Idea Crushers** should not be underestimated:

- Corporate politics
- Environment
- Fear of change
- Addicted to routine or habit
- Timing
- Fear of failure
- Logic
- Ignoring your gut
- Imposed limitations

- Lack of diversity

- Doing the same thing repeatedly while expecting different results

- Fear of the unknown

- Red tape

- Clinging to the "What is"

Einstein said: "If at first the idea is not absurd, then there is no hope for it".

Do not, however, underestimate the importance of timing. Leonardo da Vinci had some ideas similar to what we today know as a helicopter and submarine. The ideas were great, the timing wrong. The required technology was not available at the time the idea crossed his mind. Selling the idea and getting adoption of an idea can also be a challenge. The first time for anyone to use something or to try something new, is daunting, but the more you use or do it, the easier it becomes. Just break the ice.

An idea must fill a need for it to be accepted and/or adopted. Every idea has a lifespan, it does not last forever and it has a sell-by date. The typewriter and record player were great ideas at the time. Now they are retro novelty items at best. The tape recorder is no longer in use.

Ideas leap from one to another. Shamelessly borrow ideas from everywhere. One idea leads to another and before you know it, you have something like the fallen-domino effect. View every idea as a learning opportunity. Ideas no longer live solitary existences. Re-tooling ideas that already exist is not plagiarism – that is how the world works.

An idea needs to turn into a movement. Only the strongest ideas survive. Great ideas happen when you are not trying too hard – in the shower, in the bath, bedtime. Great ideas often start as fragile thoughts. New perspectives can come from anywhere. Information, no matter how beautifully it is packaged or re-packaged, does not equal an idea.

An idea should ideally lead to action and address a need.

Use information but do not be a slave to information. Find new sources of information and learning. It is first about quantity and then about quality. Look for patterns and trends – they will inspire insights. Ideas must be adopted for them to be viewed as being successful. You can have the best idea in the world, but if nobody else thinks so, then it remains just an idea. Test solutions and if they do not work – find alternatives. The sharing of ideas across cultures and generations will require a sophisticated degree of CQ.

A few more thoughts...

Old view – from...	New view – to...
Ideas come from scattered thoughts	Ideas come from deep domain knowledge and scattered thoughts
Current understanding of creativity and innovation does not deliver what it has promised	There is a need for new methodologies, frameworks, techniques and tools for understanding and implementing creativity and innovation
Focus is on managing ideas as a process	The focus is on how entertainers, artists, scientists, designers, engineers and the rest of us can transform our ideas into something that has value
Ideas are generated to meet needs	Ideas are generated to determine what is truly meaningful to people
Make innovation risk-free and predictable	Creativity is a practice that harnesses uncertainty – find the opportunity contained within the uncertainty

Reflections

- Ideas may come out of the blue, but it takes a lot of hard work to transform the idea into a creative product

- Organisations must create "idea factories" and environments that allow for ideas to be expressed, e.g. a tolerance for risk, allowing people the freedom to express their ideas

- First quantity and then quality

- A vast number of ideas should be generated, and the best should be implemented

- There are idea crushers – work around them

- There are sufficient idea generators and methodologies, techniques and tools to use in order to generate ideas

Chapter 6

The Creative Process

Does creativity just happen, or can it be willed/orchestrated/manipulated/controlled?

The creative process refers to the different phases which an individual goes through to reach his/her envisaged creative goal. In this respect various authors identify different phases. Some identify four phases, namely preparation, incubation, insight and testing while others identify the phases as: orientation, preparation, incubation, illumination and verification.

Guilford[52, 53] viewed as one of the pioneers of creativity research, lists the same processes as preparation, incubation, and instead of illumination, describes the same process as inspiration. He concludes this process with evaluation or verification, and defines the steps briefly as follows:

- Preparation: gaining the necessary skills and knowledge

- Incubation: leaving the problem in the unconscious mind

- Inspiration: when the way forward becomes clear

- Verification: develop and evaluate insight at this final stage

Some focus on the illumination stage and state that sudden illumination usually seems to emerge weeks after a person has been living with a problem. Others express the opinion that the creative process builds on preparation, incubation, illumination and verification to achieve meaningful results. The creative process depends on knowledge and experience that lead to new knowledge. Knowledge, however, is only a means to an end. **Most express the view that the creative process could involve many failures along the way to finding new ideas.**

It is vitally important that the problem is properly defined and what needs to be solved is well formulated. A properly defined problem is the starting point of the creative journey.

The following is an integrated view of the creative process:

- **Phase 1 – Orientation:** The problem has to be identified, well-formulated and defined: What needs to be solved?

- **Phase 2 – Preparation:** Gather all the relevant information – employing formal and informal methods ranging from informal interviews, formal interviews and focus groups, reading articles, internal organisation documents and conducting formal research: What is available and what still needs to be researched?

- **Phase 3 – Idea generation/ideation/ideaneering:** Make use of the methodologies, frameworks, techniques and tools included in this book – refer to the Ideas section.

- **Phase 4 – Incubation:** A period when the problem solver comes up against a wall with no solution in sight. The problem is deferred, and the problem solver carries on with other activities. This may last a few days, weeks, months or even years. Nevertheless, there is a readiness to receive information pertinent to the problem, and incubation frequently culminates in the illumination phase.

- **Phase 5 – Illumination:** Often also referred to as the **Aha!** moment or **Eureka** moment when one has a general idea of how to solve the problem. Select the best possible solutions posed by the selected methodologies, frameworks, techniques and tools.

- **Phase 6 – Verification/Evaluation:** The final step is to verify the solution that has been discovered, i.e. to determine whether the solution fits the problem situation. Insight must be developed and evaluated in this final stage – **build a prototype.**

- **Phase 7 – Implementation:** If the prototype is accepted – start production and formulate an implementation and adoption strategy: scale as soon as possible.

> Refer to and integrate this process with the SCAMPER and SCRAPBOARDS process as stated on page 103. Create your own process.

Obviously not all creative processes follow these phases exactly. But should the creative process necessarily be related to problem solving?

Writing a song can be an intense process, but it can hardly be described as problem solving. As you can see, although problem solving can be highly creative, all forms of creativity are by no means equivalent to problem solving.

Once the context for creativity is set, creative thinking and the application of CQ can be introduced in a few ways. Organisations should ideally select several techniques, methodologies, frameworks and tools to develop the CQ of their employees.

It is thus clear that a few alternative options can be considered when investigating the context in which creative thinking and problem-solving skills and techniques to enhance CQ can be developed and applied.

Creative problem solving (CPS) remains one of the best techniques to trigger, ignite and direct creative thoughts. Consciously work through the creativity methodologies, frameworks, techniques and tools selected to assist you to develop and improve your CQ. The idea is to ultimately assist individuals to develop their CQ to such an extent that they become secure in their creative ability to effectively deal with the uncertainty and stress in an increasingly VUCA world.

Reflections

- Most creatives engage in some sort of a process prior to producing their creative gifts

- The painter commences by deciding what he is going to paint, the musician by selecting a topic for a song, the writer by selecting a theme for the story to be told

- All creative outputs do not necessarily have to solve a problem

- The creative process is not one which is cast in stone

- You have the freedom of choice to select the elements of a variety of creative processes to formulate and design your own unique creative process

Chapter 7

Creativity Toolkit and Grab-Pack!

Can CQ be developed through the use of methodologies, frameworks, techniques and tools?

Take a conscious decision to become more creative. The following section will provide you with the methodologies, frameworks, techniques and tools that will not only assist you to develop your CQ but will also assist you to build your creative confidence. This section will guide you and enable you to apply them, play around with them and experiment with how effectively they can be utilised while having fun. Exercise your creative muscle and focus to enhance your CQ by regularly engaging with some of the hands-on exercises in the book that will provide you with functional skills for enhancing and developing your creativity. You need to start to see, feel, communicate, build, connect, navigate, synthesise and integrate the skills obtained during these exercises and apply them in your professional as well as in your personal life. These exercises will assist you to unleash, re-discover and re-channel your inherent and latent creative potential.

You need to acquire the agility to shift from the playful and silly (making a wearable piece of jewellery from tape or pipe cleaners) to being able to express real business challenges utilising divergent thinking, making use of only triangles, circles and squares. You need to become aware of your intuition and learn to tap into a heightened awareness of your surroundings.

You need to find your creative flow.

When are you at your best? Are you a chicken (morning person), hornbill (afternoon person) or owl (evening person)? When do you optimally perform? When are you most energetic? Actively identify and explore new areas of interest. Pluck up the courage and begin to apply creativity to your work. Take the leap from inspiration to action. Start by designing calculated quick wins and celebrate them with big brag sessions.

Consciously make the decision to be creative. You need to evolve from a blank space to insight. The creative process will assist and guide you to get there. Consciously use the creative process as a guideline to inspire. It may take some time at first. Add what you can. Cultivate a mindset of possibility. Seek to find and discover new options.

Creativity exercises will boost and assist to develop your CQ. This book aims to help you to re-discover what you already have: the capacity to imagine. You will access your prior knowledge and these exercises will help you to unleash and tap into what you don't know you already know. This book aims to unleash your inner Da Vinci, Einstein, Picasso, Sekoto, Barnard or Freddie Mercury. That potential which you carefully locked away the moment you were told that you weren't a talented artist, musician, writer, scientist or singer. When you were compared to a preconceived standard, that moment when the joy of doing, experimenting and discovery was simply taken away from you. That specific incident which robbed you of the joy of participating and exploring for the mere pleasure of it. That moment when already limited views and mindsets curbed your natural creative expressions by boxing them in. Theoretical facts will be given to contextualise some of the exercises. This book will take you through a selection of good old-fashioned pen-and-paper exercises. Make lots of notes. If you really want to go digital, try Siri and Evernote should you have access to them.

Leonardo da Vinci has been selected as being the most creative person of all times. His creative ability reached over many different domains and he was a lifelong and prolific learner. How did he do it? What was the secret to his seemingly endless supply of creative insights? Michael Gelb lists the steps to be followed to try and think like the most creative mastermind ever. View these steps as your launch pad for your creative journey.

How to think like Leonardo da Vinci

Michael Gelb[54] lists the following steps to try and think like Leonardo da Vinci[55]:

Curiosita:

Cultivate a curious approach to life and an unrelenting quest for continuous learning! Read, something you would not usually read, try a new recipe, drink an unfamiliar cocktail, create your own cocktail, draw something, boldly go where you have never gone before, reach for the force within, find your own Big Bang!

Dimostrazione:

A commitment to test knowledge through experience, persistence, and a willingness to learn from mistakes! Make mistakes, learn from them, fix them fast. Try and try again. Be kind to yourself.

Sensazione:

The continual refinement of the senses, especially sight, as the means to enliven experience! Smell the roses, smell the coffee and smell the grass. Touch to discover new textures. Listen to music you don't usually listen to. View things from different angles – from the top, from the bottom or from the side. Learn to be fully engaged!

Sfumato:

(Literally "Going up in smoke") A willingness to embrace ambiguity, paradox and uncertainty! Creativity involves a great deal of uncertainty. Having to navigate the opportunities contained in a VUCA world puts human creativity to the test like never before in the history of humankind!

Arte/Scienza:

The development of balance between science and art, logic and imagination. Combine elements from different genres and spheres in order to solve needs. The interconnected world is a creative combination fusing the science of technology with the art of communication.

Corpolalita:

The cultivation of grace, ambidexterity, fitness and poise! A healthy body harbours a healthy mind. Movement enhances creativity. The habits of great minds were studied and most of them were renowned for their walking habits. Whatever you do – just keep on walking!

Connessione:

A recognition of and appreciation for the interconnectedness of all things and phenomena. Systems thinking! Utilise the benefits of a modern connected life to your advantage. Facebook, Instagram, LinkedIn and various other platforms connect us all!

Chapter 7: Creativity Toolkit and Grab-Pack!

Divergent thinking and convergent thinking

Look at the following three images and write down next to them or underneath them what you see. Do not think about it for too long.

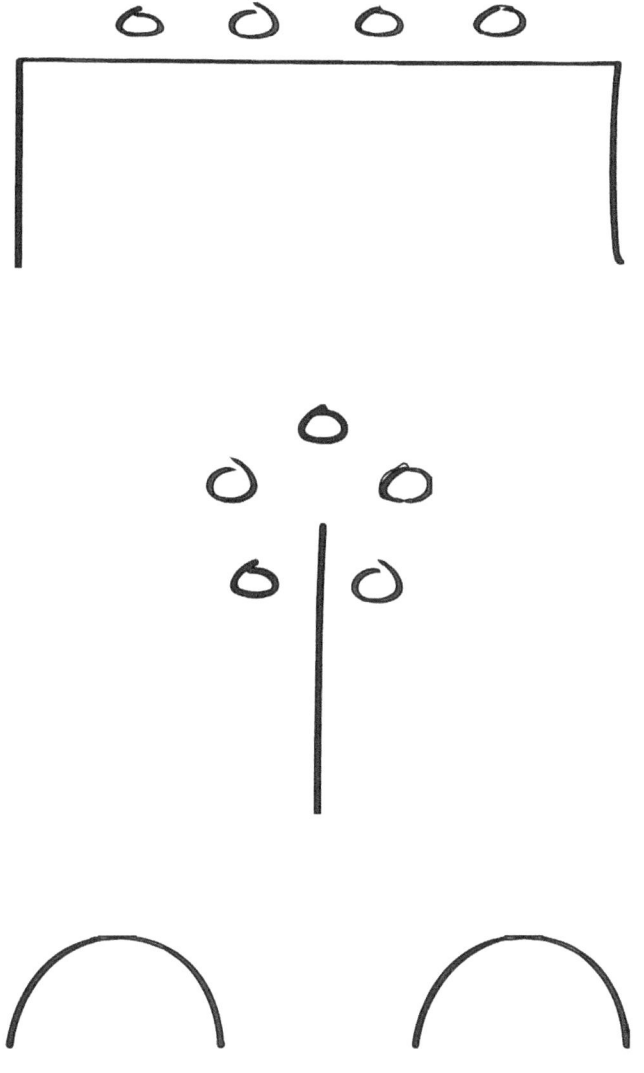

Possible Answers

The first image:

> **Convergent response:** A table with objects on it
> **Divergent response:** A foot with toes

The second image:

> **Convergent response:** A flower
> **Divergent response:** A lollipop breaking into pieces

The third image:

> **Convergent response:** Two igloos
> **Divergent response:** Two haystacks on flying carpets

Divergent and Convergent Thinking explained…

Creativity is not easily distinguished from intelligence, wisdom, ingenuity, insight, or intuition and all terms used to describe creative behaviours. Guilford's[56] distinction between convergent and divergent thinking has perhaps had the most influential effect on how our understanding of creativity has developed.

Barron[57] and Guilford[58] have identified two essential components of creative thought:

1. Divergent thinking (thinking out of the box!)

2. Cognitive Complexity/Convergent thinking (linking thinking to what is known/logical inference)

Divergent Thinking

This concept, also known as lateral thinking, has been made famous by Edward de Bono.[59, 60] It is characterised by the production of several unconventional or unusual solutions to problems or answers to questions. This is applied to problems or questions that have no "correct" solutions or answers. In contrast, problems or questions needing an answer from existing knowledge or logical inference, requires convergent thinking.

Divergent thinking has three components:

1. **Idea fluency** (the total number of solutions or answers you can come up with in a given time)

2. **Flexibility** (the number of times that you can switch your ideas between various categories)

3. **Originality** (the novelty or unconventionality of your ideas)

Good old-fashioned mind maps also enhance divergent thinking. Pen-and-pencil mind maps are fun to use but there are a few digital tools that can be used.

Cognitive Complexity/Convergent Thinking

Cognitive Complexity/Convergent Thinking results in a response that links the image of what we see to something that is known.

Barron[61] stated that creative individuals come in all ages and sizes, but visionary wisdom does seem to require a preliminary finely articulated and complex intellectual structure as well as deep intuition and empathy. Traditional institutions and organisations are known to have little tolerance for divergent thinkers and will not easily accommodate such individuals.

Corporate control systems limit creativity through their dependence on convergent thinking. Convergent thinking concentrates on clear problems and provides well-known solutions quickly. It thrives on focus. Interestingly, evidence exists that in group situations, a dissenting minority will tend to think divergently, whereas the majority will be convergent thinkers who feel less of a need to think around the problem.

Divergent thinking focuses on broadening, i.e. diverging the context of decision making. It places enormous value on getting the questions right, and then relinquishes control to conventional convergent thinking processes. Divergent thinking thrives as much on the broad search as on the focused search. It concentrates as much on careful observation of the facts as on their interpretation.

There is however a need for both convergent and divergent thinking skills. Divergent production abilities do not represent all creative aspects of intelligence. Conversely, convergent production assists in rationalising creativity. There is a use and need for both divergent and convergent thinking. Some creatives are better at generating ideas while others are better at carrying them out. Divergent thinking skills are required to produce ideas while convergent thinking skills are required to apply and implement these ideas in the workplace. Modern organisations such as King Price and Missing Link encourage divergent thinking but they also realise the role of convergence in order to implement their business strategies.

Adequate preparation, deadlines and the correct environment will support divergent thinking. Some concentrate more on the process of divergent thinking while others place greater focus on divergent and convergent thinking techniques.

The divergent process will be assisted in selecting people with a high tolerance for ambiguity and uncertainty. There should be time to reflect and to engage in dialogues for the divergent thinkers to familiarise themselves with their materials and with the situation. Divergent thinkers seek tough and important problems to solve, or they will lose interest. They also emphasise that divergent thinkers need alternative resources at their disposal. Divergent thinkers must be in an environment where they can be allowed to discover things, yet they also need deadlines. Senior management should be willing to put their reputation on the line. There will be many challenges on the way and senior management should be available to address these challenges.

There are some guidelines to consider when engaging divergent and convergent thinking. Divergent thinking requires that judgement should be deferred. People want to know that their ideas will be given a fair hearing. The more ideas generated, the higher the probability that some good ideas will be produced. "Hitchhiking" on another's idea, combining and modifying existing ideas, drawing the ideas and thinking about the impossible will stimulate divergent thinking.

Being systematic, developing evaluative measures, using intuition and questioning everything assists convergent thinking. Assess the risk of ideas generated and rank alternative solutions if required.

> Convergent thinking leads one to arrive at a correct, conventional answer whereas divergent thinking involves generating many novel answers and solutions. Start looking at things and try and imagine alternative options. What could they be? Imagine…

Divergent thinking exercises

Choose two or more of the following common items and describe as many uses for each as you can. From what you've learned about creativity, be creative in your answers. Which ones are more difficult to come up with ideas for? Why do you think this?

- paper clip (if you haven't tried this one already)
- old shoe
- sheet of paper
- pencil
- paper bag
- toothbrush

Translating your ideas into pictures is possible. Drawing enables you to see your thoughts. You are not entering an art competition. You merely need to be able to draw what you are thinking. You need to think in pictures. Anything you need to draw can be drawn by utilising the five basic shapes. Everything you ever need to draw can be de-constructed into five basic shapes: a line, a square, a circle, a triangle and an irregular shape Dan Roam (in Kelley and Kelley)[62] calls a blob. If you are harbouring the notion that you cannot draw, think again. Give it a go. Practice makes perfect!

The Triangle Test (The easiest way to develop and improve your CQ)

Take the ordinary triangle. Add a simple square and it becomes a house. Use a triangle as basis. How many pictures/images can you create in a minute? Do this exercise on a regular basis. Challenge yourself to improve your score after every attempt. The idea is to be able to draw as many pictures as possible and to continually improve on how many you can draw.

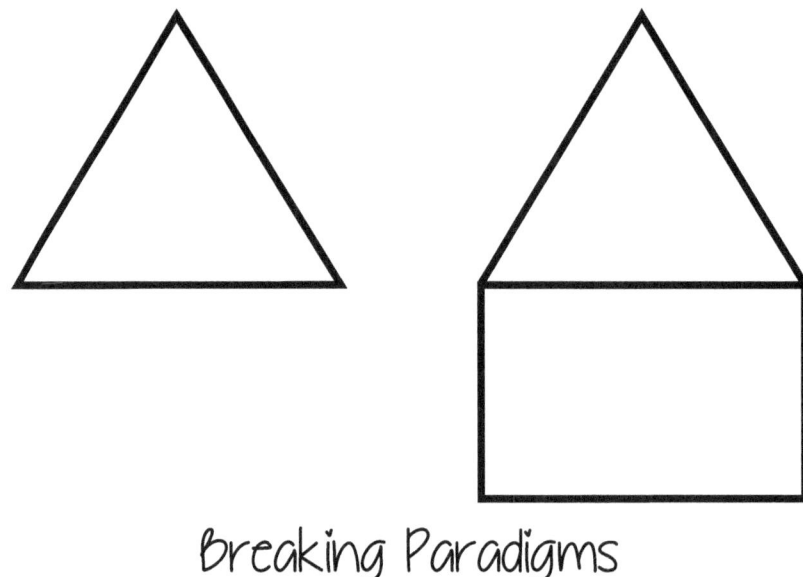

Breaking Paradigms

Leaders and managers will now more than ever before have to focus on breaking paradigms rather than using conventional wisdom. Changing from conventional thinking to producing paradigm-breaking ideas can also be achieved by using creative problem-solving (CPS) techniques. Using problem-solving techniques can in turn enhance and develop CQ.

Organisations should stimulate creative thinking and problem-solving skills in order to produce paradigm-breaking ideas. This can be achieved by creating the right context to turn these ideas into applicable business solutions. A creative climate for creative problem solving and for the development of methodologies, frameworks, techniques and tools to enhance one's CQ can be developed in many ways. Of these, problem-solving sessions or workshops have proven to be the most successful.

In order to run effective creative problem-solving and CQ enhancement training sessions, the climate and culture within the organisation must be such that the company encourages creative thinking. The following actions can be taken to ensure participant involvement in creative problem-solving sessions and commitment to taking ownership to develop their CQ:

- Ensure participant safety. Employees can only be encouraged to think creatively if they are not afraid of criticism or punishment. For example, if a project fails and the champion is in fear of losing his job, he/she might never risk thinking creatively again.

- Employees should be encouraged to challenge their assumptions and perceptions regarding procedures, products, services and processes. They should examine procedures that "have always been done that way". This attitude will not thrive in the context of the 4IR.

- Managers should encourage "visioning" and "visualisation". Creative thinkers look into the future and visualise where they would like to be in five or ten years' time. This can be applied to the company as a whole or to a department or section or to products, services, procedures and processes. The reality of how AI, robotics, VR and IoTs will impact the NWOW should ideally form part of the vision.

- Establish a climate of excellence. Creative ideas must be implemented effectively in order to succeed. Managers should ensure that employees are committed to achieving a first-rate performance. This can be undertaken by developing achievable objectives (both as an organisation and as individuals) and by producing a strategy for fulfilling them.

- Employ diverse people. By upsetting the status quo, it encourages people to look at situations from different perspectives instead of a "corporate viewpoint". This may not necessarily be comfortable for management, but it can help the company produce some excellent innovative ideas.

- Allow people to spend time to research and develop their pet projects. For example, the Post-it-note was developed by 3M because the company had allowed its inventor, Arthur Fry, to spend 15 percent of working time on researching the concept.

- The development and application of creativity resulting from utilising latent or acquired CQ needs to be supported by senior management. Often, managers will articulate their support but will not enact it. They should provide enough resources and training, encouragement for developing new ideas, time to work on pet projects and/or financial support.

- Encourage an atmosphere of enjoyment and fun. Creative thought could be greatly enhanced if participants are enjoying themselves. An appropriate atmosphere could be created by reducing distractions and enhancing relaxation. Play and learn – learn while you play should ideally form part of the process employed.

- Develop creative problem-solving teams that can work together and develop trust in one another. Problem-solving teams will be more effective if the participants have the same goals and are supported by a trained facilitator. Group members who share goal congruence will work together towards their objectives rather than working with hidden agendas and conflicting interests, which will ultimately reduce the efficiency of the group. In addition, the group will work together more effectively if supported by a competent facilitator. Such a facilitator can firstly assist the group in reaching its objectives and secondly assist the group to look at the situation from different perspectives by using a variety of creative problem-solving techniques.

The above requirements need to be in place to establish the climate required for creative problem-solving sessions and when creativity workshops are presented and are based on the work of Levesque[63], VanGundy[64], Von Oech[65] & Von Oetinger[66] as integrated by De Jager.

> Divergence (an overview was provided earlier in this book) is another way in which a framework for creative problem solving is created. This includes the deferment of judgement, using new ideas as solution stimuli and encouraging equal participation. Osborn[67], the father of creative problem-solving and brainstorming, advocates two essential guiding principles: Firstly, the idea-

generation phase should take place without any analysis or evaluation. Secondly, the quantity of ideas will ultimately yield quality. In other words, the more ideas generated, the more likely it is that the participants will produce some good quality ideas (ideas were discussed at an earlier stage in this book and some more thoughts with regard to ideas will be shared at a later stage in the book).

It is important to have a relaxed and playful atmosphere, get into a humorous frame of mind because it not only loosens you or people up, it enhances your creativity. Humour enhances creative thinking. Humour can help to stretch a person's thinking and facilitate a change in his or her mindset. It can also force people to combine ideas that have not been associated together before. In addition, humour helps to relax people and encourages them to be less serious, thus reducing one of the blocks to creativity – that of feeling foolish or the fear of making a mistake.

The process of preparing and planning a creative problem-solving session is critical to its success. Bad preparation, a poorly structured agenda and poor time keeping can greatly reduce the efficiency and effectiveness of meetings. Teams are an important part of organisational life. They are formed to solve problems, to realise opportunities and to undertake and supervise projects. A team that is creative can develop new and creative ideas and thus add value to the organisation. The leader or manager, or if you read this book and you are not the leader or manager but someone who is serious about creativity and CQ, should try some of these techniques and see what happens. It can just be fun. If not, then you have at least tried.

Creative Problem-Solving (CPS) in action

A brief explanation of a few creative problem-solving techniques, based on the work of De Jager[68], McFadzean[69] and VanGundy[70, 71, 72, 73] will now be given.

Using paradigm-preserving techniques: brainstorming

This technique contains the basic idea as it is. Brainstorming relies on the absence of evaluation in the idea generation phase. Moreover, freewheeling is encouraged so that an extensive list of ideas can be generated. The group members should be allowed to communicate an idea, however mundane, strange or wild, to the rest of the group. A great solution could stem from an idea that seemed totally impractical.

Using paradigm-stretching techniques: object stimulation and metaphors

This technique views the idea from a different perspective. Object stimulation is a technique to generate ideas that can be used to explore the problem space as well as to enhance solution development. The technique encourages participants to view the situation from a different perspective by using unrelated stimuli.

The objects chosen can range from garden tools to animals to organisations to pictures. This technique requires much more imagination than the paradigm-preserving techniques and may therefore cause some discomfort to some team members who feel that it may be "a waste of time".

Metaphors can be used to create a fantasy situation so that a new perspective of the problem can be gained. Various types of metaphors useful for problem solving and opportunity finding exist. These include metaphors of nature, vehicle metaphors, creational metaphors, the journey metaphor, and so on. Again, this method requires some imagination by the group. The development of metaphors, however, may be difficult for some people and will require practice. Nevertheless, once it has been mastered the results produced can be very creative.

In order to make both paradigm-stretching and paradigm-breaking techniques effective, the group must be experienced in the use of creative problem-solving techniques. They need to trust their fellow participants and their facilitator and should have a vested interest in the outcome of the session.

Using paradigm-breaking techniques: wishful thinking (What if...)

This technique assists participants to use their wildest imagination and fantasies. Badly structured and open-ended problems may require more creative thinking. Paradigm-breaking techniques can help participants to develop fantasies that may aid in the novel generation of ideas.

Wishful thinking forces participants to look at a "perfect future". By using this method, it allows group members to develop an attainable goal. Moreover, it can increase their motivation and help to change their perspective.

This is not an easy technique to facilitate because some of the fantasies can be difficult (or impractical) to develop into practical solutions. The participants and the facilitator should have worked together before and have developed a high degree of trust. If this technique is used properly, different perspectives can be produced that would not have been developed through using paradigm-preserving techniques.

Creative problem-solving techniques help to structure the group process so that novel ideas can be generated and developed into practical solutions. The use of group creative problem solving will only be effective, however, if the organisation itself has a creative culture. Creative problem solving requires considering who is solving the problem, how it is solved, and how the solution is implemented. Finding a good solution is not enough; in most cases, creative problem solving starts with having relevant expertise.

Creative problem-solving sessions are only one of many techniques, methodologies, frameworks and tools to be deployed to assist you and teams to put your CQ to play to assist you to re-imagine, re-invent and re-create the future.

More creative thinking and problem-solving methodologies, frameworks, techniques and tools will still be discussed. The idea is to use them as is or to cleverly design new combinations in order to address or solve the prevailing and pressing challenge, problem or produce a creative product, service or outcome. Brainstorming was the first of the three CPS techniques discussed. More information with regard to brainstorming will now be shared.[74, 75]

The Step-by-Step Guide to Brainstorming[76]

> Brainstorming can be an effective way to generate lots of ideas and then determine which idea(s) best solve(s) the problem. Brainstorming is most effective with larger groups of people and should be performed in a relaxed environment. If participants feel free to be silly, they'll stretch their minds more and therefore produce more creative ideas.

In order to brainstorm, you will need a chalkboard (if there are any still left in the world), a white-board or lots of Post-it notes (a valuable creativity tool) and a wall, window or door.

Brainstorming works best when you have a larger group of diverse people. If you are a division in a company, invite people from other divisions to participate. Try to get as varied a group as possible to participate – this will result in the widest and most creative range of ideas.

Step by Step

1. Define your problem/challenge (please note that the word "problem" is not necessarily negative – your problem could be "We need a new product for the Christmas season" or "How can we effectively use our departmental budget surplus for this year?"). Write out your problem concisely and make sure that everyone understands the problem and agrees with the way it is worded. There is no need to put a lot of restrictions on your problem at this time.

2. Give yourselves a time limit – we recommend around 25 minutes, but experience will show how much time is required. Larger groups may need more time to "extract" everyone's ideas.

3. Everyone must shout out solutions to the problem while one person writes them down. There must be ABSOLUTELY NO CRITICISING OF IDEAS. No matter how daft, how impossible or how silly an idea is, it must be written down. Laughing is to be encouraged. Criticism is not. Why? Because you want to encourage the free flow of ideas and as soon as

participants of the brainstorming session begin to fear criticism of their ideas, they'll stop generating ideas. Moreover, ideas that at first seem silly may prove to be very good or may lead to ideas that are very good.

4. Once your time is up, select the five ideas that you like best. Make sure everyone involved in the brainstorming session agrees.

5. Write down about five criteria for judging which ideas best solve your problem. Criteria should start with the word "should", for example, "it should be cost effective", "it should be legal", "it should be possible to finish before July 15", amongst others.

6. Give each idea a score of 0 to 5 points depending on how well it meets each criterion. Once all the ideas have been scored for each criterion, add up the scores.

7. The idea with the highest score will best solve your problem. But you should keep a record of all your best ideas and their scores in case your best idea turns out not to be workable.

The following is a very short and effective brainstorming tool.

Alex Osborn's creative thinking tool:[77]

BRAINSTORMING

1. Quantity Yields Quality
2. No Judgement
3. Hitchhiking
4. Freewheeling

How can this process be improved? Respect those individuals who generate more ideas when they are alone. Inviting them to a brainstorming session may ignite their imaginations but you need to find a way to harness the ideas generated by the solitary ideaneers. Maybe informal face-to-face coffee sessions where you just engage in casual conversation can assist to mine these ideas.

Think in opposites: silent brainstorming as opposed to shouting the ideas out. Give each person at least five Post-it notes. Let them write the ideas on Post-it notes. Let them place them on the wall. Cluster similar ideas. This will give the more silent and introverted delegates an opportunity to also express their ideas.

Brainstorming Exercises

In a small group, or on your own, choose one of the following topics and describe what would be required to accomplish you goal. Be as detailed as you like. Use your imagination. Write your ideas down, but do not evaluate them until you have finished brainstorming (i.e. run out of ideas). Think of wild ideas. Think of many ideas. Build on ideas.

- Write and present a report on school safety
- Install a porch at your house
- Purchase five new computers for your office
- Live on the surface of the moon
- Discover who killed John F. Kennedy/Steve Biko
- Go on a two-week vacation to another country

Bruce Nussbaum[78] expresses the opinion that we need to replace brainstorming with what he calls "magic circles". These are environments where two or three smart people who trust each other can come together and "play" at connecting disparate dots of knowledge in an open-ended kind of game. Look at the innovations that have changed our lives: Google, Facebook, Match.com; ZipCar, Amazon, 3M's Post-its – even jazz and rock & roll. In each case, there was a small group of people working together in a 'playground' setting – a magic circle. That circle can be in a lab, a school, a conference room – anywhere that you can have space, time and permission to improvise. This is the type of setting we need for innovation in an era of constant, cascading change.

A brainteaser to get you boiling

Here is a brainteaser to stretch your paradigm:

Each question below contains the initials of the words that will make it a correct phrase. Find the missing words.

FOR EXAMPLE: 7 D in a W.

ANSWER: 7 Days in a Week. Just write the answer next to the phrase or on a piece of paper. Make sure you number it correctly.

1. 26 L of the A   _____
2. 7 W of the W   _____
3. 1001 A N   _____
4. 12 S of the Z   _____
5. 54 C in the D [with the J]   _____
6. 9 P in the SS   _____
7. 88 P K   _____
8. 0 D C at which W F   _____
9. 18 H on a G C   _____
10. 90 D in a R A   _____
11. 200 D for P G in M   _____
12. 8 S on a S S   _____
13. 3 B M [S H T R]   _____
14. 4 C in a L   _____
15. 24 H in a D   _____
16. 1 W on a U   _____
17. 11 P on a F T   _____
18. 1000 W that a P is W   _____
19. 29 D in F in a L Y   _____
20. 64 S on a C   _____
21. 40 D and N of the G F   _____

Answers:

1.	26 L of the A	(letters of the alphabet)
2.	7 W of the W	(wonders of the ancient world)
3.	1001 A N	(Arabian nights)
4.	12 S of the Z	(signs of the zodiac)
5.	54 C in the D [with the J]	(cards in a deck with jokers)
6.	9 P in the SS	(planets in the solar system)
7.	88 P K	(piano keys)
8.	0 D C at which W F	(degrees Celsius at which water freezes)
9.	18 H on a G C	(holes in a golf course)
10.	90 D in a R A	(degrees in a right angle)
11.	200 D for P G in M	(dollars for passing "go" in monopoly)
12.	8 S on a S S	(sides on a stop sign)
13.	3 B M [S H T R]	(blind mice, see how they run!)
14.	4 C in a L	(cups in a litre)
15.	24 H in a D	(hours in a day)
16.	1 W on a U	(wheel on a unicycle)
17.	11 P on a F T	(players on a football team)
18.	1000 W that a P is W	(words that a picture is worth)
19.	29 D in F in a L Y	(days in February in a leap year)
20.	64 S on a C	(squares on a chessboard)
21.	40 D and N of the G F	(days and nights of the great flood)

How many did you get right? You can only recognise the letter phrase if you have been exposed to the situation or if you have prior knowledge about what the letters represent in your memory. Then and then only can you fill in the blanks.

How many of those did you get right by either using your imagination or common sense without having any prior memory of the subject at hand?

Chapter 7: Creativity Toolkit and Grab-Pack!

Language is a powerful change tool. A funky name also ignites interest in or sells products. Playing around with words is a wonderful way to stimulate creative thinking. Use the words below in sentences to give them meaning.

Dilly Dictionary

Invent a definition for each of the following imaginary words. State what type of word each is (noun, verb, etc.) and use each one in a sample sentence. Any SA words?

1. swage

2. ectorthic

3. rabelate

4. corple

5. mander

6. contority

7. sarmenish

8. onderage

9. barble

10. trummer

The Discontinuity Principle

The more you are used to something, the less stimulating it is for our thinking.

When you disrupt your thought patterns, those ideas that create the greatest stimulus to our thinking do so because they force us to make new connections in order to comprehend the situation. Roger van Oech[79, 80, 81] calls this a *"Whack on the Side of the Head"*, and Edward de Bono[82, 83] coined a new word, PO, which stands for *"Provocative Operation"*.

> Try programming interruptions into your day. Change working hours, get to work in a different way, listen to a different radio station, read some magazines or books you wouldn't normally read, try a different recipe, watch a TV programme or film you wouldn't normally watch. Perhaps brush your teeth with your other hand, move your watch to your other arm, sit in a different seat in meetings or at the dining table, mix and match your clothes combinations, use the mouse with your other hand or start a new hobby.

Provocative ideas are often stepping stones that get us thinking about other ideas.

Abutting ideas next to each other, such that their friction creates new thought-paths, is a technique that flourishes in the East (for example, haiku poetry) but causes discomfort in Western thinking.

More Creativity Crunches

- Choose a common word and quickly list as many rhymes for it as possible. Now compose a poem, using as many of the rhymes as you can.
- Make a list of several things that frighten you as an adult. Now choose one and write on it for fifteen minutes.
- If you could have fifty of anything (except money) what would it be? Why?
- Write for ten minutes, in answer to the following question: If you could be 3 cm tall for a day, what place would you most like to explore? Why?
- Come up with an idea for a creativity exercise.
- Write a 100-word short story without using the letter "e".
- Open a dictionary to a random page and jot down the first word you read. Do this ten times. Now compose a poem, any style, using as many of the ten words as possible.
- Write ten fortunes you would not want to find in a fortune cookie.
- Write the worst possible opening sentence for a story or novel.

Be the Inventor

An inventor is a person who makes things that have not been made before. Usually an invention solves a problem. Think about the following inventions and recreate the problem that may have existed that lead to the invention. Be unconventional or off the wall, be serious or logical, but be creative. Why do you think they invented the:

- Light bulb?
- Cell phone?
- Rubik's cube?
- French fries (chips)?
- Automobile?
- Pocket calculator?

Now that you've played with the thoughts that may have gone through the mind of an inventor, you are ready to be the inventor. Choose one of the problems below and describe the material you would need, and the steps you would take to create your invention. How would you go about inventing?

- a trap to catch a mouse without killing it
- an appliance that will make toast, boil water
- a pen whose ink fades after eight months so you can reuse your notebooks
- printers' ink that doesn't get on your hands
- tires that don't wear out
- disposable underwear

Mnemonics:

The following two words: SCAMPER and SCRAPBOARDS are two words that were constructed using and combining different creativity techniques. These two words can either be used as is or you can try and create your own word by combining creativity techniques that are applicable to your specific situation.

SCAMPER:[84]

S: SUBSTITUTE	(Sweetener instead of sugar)
C: COMBINE	(McDonald's Happy Meals – food and toys)
A: ADOPT	(Start using Uber instead of taxis; Airbnb)
M: MAGNIFY/MODIFY	(McDonald's Supersize Meals)
P: PUT TO OTHER USES	(Milton to keep water of plants fresher)
E: ELIMINATE	(Self-driving cars)
R: REARRANGE/REVISE	(Shelves in shops)

*First introduced by Alex Osborn and adapted by Rob Eberle.[85]

SCRAPBOARDS:

- **Spot** the problem
- **Collect** all information
- **Revisit** the problem
- **Ask** others what they see
- **Park** the problem
- **Brainstorm** (Refer to page 94)
- **Outline** the **problem**
- **Avoid** killer phrases!
- **Record** responses
- **Draw** the situation
- **Study** all the options

SCRAPBOARDS is a process that I developed for PPC in 2014 as part of an intervention designed to establish a culture supportive of creativity and innovation.

Create your own process and find your own acronym to simplify it. It is easier than you think!

And there is more/A pocket guide:

- What is the opposite?
- What can you eliminate?
- What can you combine?
- What can you add?
- Can you change the size?
- Is there an alternative?
- What if?

The above is a pocket guide of the most used creativity and innovation guidelines.

Think in Opposites[86, 87]

Thinking in opposites is a creativity technique that can be used effectively in most creativity exercises and during most creative experiences. When all else fails: Think in Opposites.

Life today is full of wonderful paradoxes:

- A baby bottle nipple company also makes condoms. (Aren't they self-defeating?)

- A woman lives in a tree for two years to save it from being cut down and signs a book deal to tell about her experience. (Don't they cut down trees to print books?)

- Our parents had groceries delivered to their home. Then we invented malls and bought minivans to carry it all home. Now we order online for home delivery.

- "Go to your room!" used to be a childhood punishment. Now "your room" is a multi-media amphitheatre of games, music and online chat sessions.

- "All behaviour consists of opposites. Learn to see backward, inside out and upside down." [Lao Tzu, Tao Te Ching]

- The advertising industry uses opposites to capture human attention. When a form of packaging was invented to prevent dehydration of foods stored in electric freezers, advertisers came up with the oxymoron "freezer burn" to describe the problem the packaging would solve.

- By holding opposites together, we suspend our thought and our mind moves to a new level. Leonardo da Vinci believed that the first way he looked at a problem was too biased towards his usual way of seeing things. Pablo Picasso believed in opposites by stating, "Every act of creation is first of all an act of destruction."

The Opposite Formula

- The Negative Definition

    - Ask, "What isn't our problem"

- Flip-Flop Actions

    - Ask, "What would we never do?"

    www.destroyyourbusiness.com

At GE they ask, "What Internet solution can we create that will capture our existing business?"

Ask, "How can we profit from this problem?"

The "What If..." Compass

Describe your problem and then pick two opposing actions.

Stretch it... Shrink it.

Put it to music... Put it in pictures.

Combine it... Separate it.

Make it stronger... Make it weaker.

Winterise it... Summerise it.

Speed it up... Slow it down.

Make it invisible... Make it visible.

Force it... Relax it.

Make it fly... Make it float.

Raise price... Offer it free.

Magnetize it... Demagnetize it.

Jump over it... Go under it.

>Ask "What if…" for each action.

>Look for possibilities.

Select a couple of the above possibilities and list some examples to illustrate how this has been applied e.g.

Winterise it...Summerise it

Hot Milo....Cold Milo

Hot Tea...Iced Tea

Make it invisible...Make it visible

Radio...Television

The crab-pack is concluded with an exercise that will not only assess the prior knowledge of any given topic of the attending delegates but will also stretch their imaginations by asking them to imagine. Finally, some thoughts about the power of play as a creativity tool will be shared with you.

Speed Meeting

- Write a couple of questions on paper pertaining to questions regarding the prior knowledge you want to assess as well as how they view the ideal future state

- Hand it to the delegates to discuss and provide feedback on flipcharts

- The prior knowledge of the attending delegates will be assessed, their imaginations will be stretched and patterns and trends will lead to the required insights.

The Power of Play

Playing is not the exclusive domain of kids. It is a complex behaviour and learning tool that can drive and ignite the creation of life-altering technologies, products, services and companies. Playgrounds and playpens foster creativity. Organisations have realised this, and several organisations have created spaces with the intent to allow people to play and to be creative. People are given permission to play games, explore, make up new rules and discover different ways of winning. Games are the fastest moving social structure in society today. A generation raised on multiplayer video games is using their experience to create new business models in the fields of finance, education, sports, manufacturing, medicine, music and art. Playing games and learning how to design games effectively teaches people not only how to create new products and services but also how to build their own complex social systems. Games are the perfect organisational structure for learning and for unleashing creativity. Learn while you play and play while you learn. Playing and having fun spontaneously unleash latent creative potential.

Approach all the above methodologies, frameworks, techniques and tools in a playful manner. Take a conscious decision to master one technique at a time. Make time to actively engage with these techniques. Start by using the ones you are familiar with or that you are comfortable with. Then proceed to more challenging situations and environments. Everyone can be creative. Give yourself the gift of enhancing your creative confidence and improving your CQ. Don't delay. You owe it to yourself to do so! CQ can be developed through creativity methodologies, frameworks, techniques and tools!

"Creativity is intelligence at play." [Albert Einstein]

"CQ@Play = imagination in action." [Cherylene de Jager]

 # Reflections

- Methodologies, frameworks, techniques and tools can develop and enhance one's CQ
- Divergent Thinking results in more than one possibility that has to be considered while Convergent Thinking seeks the conventional answer
- Exercise to think in pictures – start with The Triangle Test and then substitute the triangles with circles, squares and rectangles
- Try some paradigm-breaking techniques – stretch your imagination – ask: **What if…**
- Acquire proper brainstorming techniques
- Play with words – use the power of language to create different points of view
- Disrupt your thought patterns by changing the way you normally do things e.g. take a different route to work
- Think in Opposites
- Combine and connect different elements from the above methodologies, frameworks, techniques and tools in order to design your own unique solution
- Most important of all: **Have fun while you are doing it!**

Chapter 8

Design Thinking

Is Design Thinking merely a tool used to ignite creativity and innovation or is it a discipline in its own right?

There are different views with regard to what Design Thinking is. Some researchers and authors are of the opinion that Design Thinking embodies a wide range of creative characteristics and the design of products and services is a critical component of business competitiveness. Design Thinking has multiple perspectives, different layers, works across projects and converts problems into opportunities.

The key components of the design process are that design should be human-centred, action-oriented, and that the designer should be mindful of the process. Design Thinking incorporates consumer insights in depth and rapid prototyping, all aimed at getting beyond assumptions that block effective solutions. The design process is one of problem finding, problem selecting, solution finding and solution selecting. Design is a collaborative effort[88] and ideas must be envisioned, "prototyped" and explored in a hands-on way.

Is design thinking a problem-solving activity? Designers use visualisation techniques, multiple representations in parallel and almost continuous evaluations and explore all aspects of problems through multiple sources and iterations. Designers should be able to apply qualitative information handling techniques applicable to many kinds of conceptual problems where complex solutions are desirable. Designers should be able to spot patterns and trends and obtain insights from the available data.

Design projects are hard to plan and control because they are a mix of a linear problem-solving process and an iterative learning process. The paradox and ambiguity are confusing at times. Some researchers and designers disagree and state that design's place in the world is lost when design is mobilised within a managerial framework. Frameworks are required to provide structure to teams that feel safe within them. Frameworks may encourage freedom to explore, starting the process from what is known. That can be the point of departure to dare to explore the unknown. Design Thinking can lead to fundamental innovation and it can require an organisation to break away from its current mental model. Corporate leaders and managers should chase the vital, elusive spark of creativity but the reality is that their organisations' structures, processes, and norms extinguish it wherever it flares up. Designers should volunteer to operate as agents of change within an organisation or project. Students need to learn design skills and ways in which to enhance their CQ.

Research practice that ignores context is doomed to misunderstanding and misrepresentations.

Design Thinking does, however, remain under-theorised and under-studied; indeed the critical rethinking of design thinking has only just begun.[89] Some prominent prophets of design thinking such as Professor Bruce Nussbaum have turned away from Design Thinking in favour of 'creative intelligence' and Johannson-Skőldberg, Woodilla and Cetinkaya[90] extend this view by stating that Design Thinking is not an enduring concept to be used in academia or the management world. A more recent view is that there is a notable shift in organisations about applying design principles to the way people work. Elements of different Design Thinking approaches are combined as opposed to just using an approach in its purest form. This approach is in large part a response to the increasing complexity of modern technology, modern business and modern connectivity.

Martin[91] predicted in 2010 that in future, most successful businesses will **balance analytical mastery, intuitive originality and creativity** in a dynamic interplay that he refers to as 'Design Thinking.' It seems as if he was able to spot a trend that is currently highly debated. The elements and themes of Design Thinking that are evident in the literature research are displayed by the basic Design Thinking model of: empathise, define, ideate, prototype and test. The basic Design Thinking model should use the following as point of reference: design is human-centred, focuses on the needs of customers, is collaborative, includes all stakeholders, is iterative and non-linear, alternates divergent and convergent thinking and ignites creativity and innovation. Human Centred Design designs with the customer in mind. The first step is to be able to empathise with the customer, to put yourself in their shoes. What is their need? What needs solving? Start by observing their behaviour by using the empathy map below and by asking the suggested questions.

Observe human behaviour (Empathy Map):

- What is the person thinking?
- What is the person seeing?
- What is the person hearing?
- What is the person feeling?
- What is the person saying?
- What is the person doing?
- What is the person creating?

The journey map below will now provide some guidelines to follow to obtain a more comprehensive view of the customer experience.

Customer Journey Map

- Change the world – change your mind
- Improve the lives of the end user
- Design for real people (empathy and human-centred design)
- Seek to understand the customer
- Update your own worldview
- Ask the right questions and if you need to – reframe the question
- Start with the end user in mind

- Consider the customer's ideal experience
- Map the customer's entire experience
- Make the customer experience tangible
- Show me
- Draw it
- The four Whiskeys and a Hotel: Why, What, Where, When and How
- Think aloud
- Describe it
- Use story boards
- Start a movement

The designer's secret to success: the prototype!

The prototype

- A good prototype tells a story
- Never go into a meeting without a prototype of some sort
- Make it real – a picture (prototype) speaks 1 000 words
- Prototypes must be cheap and rough
- One should not feel sorry for the prototype
- The prototype must represent the minimal viable product
- View the prototype as a napkin pitch
- Give yourself permission to fail
- Fail often, fail fast – learn from it – move on – fix it
- Build something, e.g. a wallet
- Start with what you like: I like…
- Then give feedback in the form of positive suggestions: What about… May I suggest/I suggest…
- Translate feedback into learning
- What doesn't work?
- Why doesn't it work? How can we make it work?
- Make corrections
- Test it until it works – until the solution addresses and solves the problem

Chapter 8: Design Thinking

- Learn to judge the success or failure not by the outcome, but by the quality of the decisions made

Design Thinking: A Twist on a Fairy Tale (or three)

Now let's select a tool and have some fun with it. One of the tools is to make use of the following four questions: What is (the present), What if (the future), What wows (prototype) and What works (co-creating the final offering). The first two questions are now utilised to provide a different take on Little Red Riding Hood (RRH).

Idea: Cherylene de Jager. Illustration: Sandra Kellerman

What is (the present): a little girl in a red cape; a mother; a sick grandmother; a suspicious wolf; a huntsman or woodcutter; a wood to walk through; a picnic basket of food to be delivered to the sick grandmother; a word of caution: do not stop and speak to strangers; RRH stopped to speak to a stranger who happened to be a talking wolf; she tells him where her grandmother lives; wolf eats grandmother; tries to eat RRH; huntsman/woodcutter kills wolf; rescues both; they live happily ever after!

The above is the story (with a few variations) as it is usually told...BUT: **What if...**

What if (future): a modern young lady suitably dressed; a mother; a grandmother at an outdoor yoga retreat; a qualified game ranger; a park to drive through; a healthy smoothie (gluten free, vegan friendly) to be delivered to the grandmother; a word of caution: do not stop in the park or get out of the car; RHH sees injured wolf; stops and gets out of the car; phones 911; 911 dispatch game ranger; game ranger arrives; game ranger calls other game rangers to assist; wolf is rescued; grandmother gets her smoothie; they live happily ever after! (And so, you continue...)

A few thoughts with regard to **What if...**

The question **What if...** challenges our understanding of the world as it is and can be. In the process of thinking about a different future, you can increase your understanding about the present as well. Sometimes **What if...** leads to radical new products or industries. Sometimes the only thing of importance is the learning process. Push yourself out of the conventional narrative and think about what might be...a powerful tool in which to kill killer phrases! A good strategy for **What if...** is to begin by looking at major trends.

What wows (prototype): Ask for feedback on both stories; assumption is that story is still relevant; incorporate feedback and present for feedback again if so required.

What works (co-create the final offering): Now is the time to make decisions as to what will satisfy the need of the user: is the traditional offering still preferred or is a new modern take on an old favourite now required?

Re-write the following fairy tales by using the above guideline. Look at the two images and use them as point of departure to give your imagination carte blanche!

Chapter 8: Design Thinking

Ideas: Cherylene de Jager. Illustrations: Sandra Kellerman

Reflections

- Experiment with and utilise Design Thinking
- Create an understanding of what Design Thinking means to you and create a definition or view as point of departure
- Select tools, frameworks, methodologies and guidelines that work for you and start to play – the more you play the easier it becomes
- Start by making use of something familiar and use the 4 questions to ignite the imagination
- Iterate until you find an acceptable solution
- Have empathy with the people whose lives you want to improve
- Don't underestimate the value of empathy
- Translate thoughts/ideas into prototypes, present prototypes, iterate until a solution is signed-off and then quickly take action
- Action and iteration are important for creativity and innovation
- Launch, sprint, do-something: act
- Cultivate a "do-something" mind-set – just get going
- Iterate with a small prototype quickly and cheaply
- Time constraints can inspire creativity
- Kodak failed to turn insights and ideas into effective action
- Build a cheap prototype – free your mind: use pipe cleaners, glue guns, Post-it notes
- Constraints and limitations fuel creative action (orange, black and white)
- We all want more staff, budget and time

- Use what already exists to get it done
- Have fun and enjoy the process – unleash your inner Da Vinci, Einstein and Picasso
- Mistakes are allowed and try, try again until you succeed!
- Design Thinking can be viewed as a tool igniting creativity and innovation or it can be viewed as an independent genre in its own right

True creativity illuminates what, without it, would never have been.

Anonymous

Chapter 9

Breakthrough Thinking

What do we need to know about breakthrough thinking?

In business, a breakthrough is often described as an idea that solves a problem or satisfies a need in an entirely new way. A breakthrough is simply that moment when you break through something that was previously limiting you. It is very often referred to as the **Aha** or **Eureka** moment.

Fox Cabane and Pollack[92] identify four styles of breakthrough thinking and state that no style of breakthrough is better or more productive than the other. The Eureka breakthrough is the moment when someone experiences a sudden, unexpected realisation. It delivers a concrete, immediately applicable answer. Metaphorical breakthroughs usually arrive as metaphors or analogies and require interpretations before they are complete. They occur as the brain connects two seemingly disparate items or ideas. Intuitive breakthroughs defy logic and explanation and tend to be more of a beginning. They allow us to make progress down a longer path. The Paradigm breakthrough is the kind of breakthrough that affects all of humanity and changes the world. It does not have any immediate concrete application. Be mindful of which kind of breakthrough comes naturally to you.

Fox Cabane and Pollack[93] also incorporate elements of cognitive neuroscience into their discussions. They explain that our brains have two modes of operation: focused mode and meandering mode. Focus mode is the executive mode that helps us get things done and is powered by the executive network (EN) of the brain and is goal and action orientated. Meandering mode is the source of creativity and innovation and is powered in the default network (DN) of the brain and is always running in the background, 24/7. This correlates with the need for an incubation period required to process ideas and thoughts. That is why I always suggest an incubation period of no less than ten but not longer than fourteen working days between the idea generation phase and the solution and evaluation phases respectively.

Fox Cabane and Pollack[94] continue and state that both modes are required for breakthroughs and therefore we must learn to switch back and forth between them. The minutes just before and after sleep can be a fertile environment for breakthroughs.

Have you ever wondered why ideas or solutions appear to you at the most unexpected moments or when you least expect them? It is when you are busy with mindless and routine tasks. Research suggests that in order to enhance creativity among chronically overworked and highly stressed professionals, their schedules should alternate between bouts of cognitively challenging high-pressure work and bouts of mindless work, e.g. washing dishes by hand, playing video games, folding laundry, doodling, cooking a meal you have cooked many times before and drawing or doodling.

Keep on walking. Walking stimulates your brain from a physical angle. Increased blood flow causes a cascade of wonderful changes in the brain, including the release of brain-derived-neurotropic factor (BDNF) and other growth factors. BDNF promotes the birth of new neurons and the formation of new synapses, and it also strengthens existing synapses. The single common habit of most famous innovators and great inventors is walking, as mentioned earlier in the book. Charles Dickens walked, Darwin walked, Beethoven walked, Einstein walked. Johnny is forever walking ...

Discover your breakthrough mojo. Consciously create opportunities where you put yourself in that environment more often. Play with your physical surroundings. Use colour, texture, music. Visualise the solution. Change the soundtrack. Dance to a different tune. The long and the short of it – the mind must be allowed to wander for breakthroughs to occur.

Constraints will set you free. I have worked with many teams where they are convinced that they do not have the time, the budget or the resources required to achieve a breakthrough or solve a problem. I then challenge them to find ways in which to creatively address these perceived constraints. Sometimes this is the first breakthrough required. In most cases at least one of these constraints could be addressed, igniting the necessary confidence to try and find creative ways in which to address the other challenges as well.

I would like to share with you not a constraint per se, but rather a brand confirmation choice which imposed a constraint by choice. I chose to wear only orange, black and white for a period of five years. The unintended consequence of this constraint enhanced my creativity in ways that I could not imagine. The constraint resulted in very creative outfits combining the three colours in very creative ways. Creative combinations and variations of the colour palette were chosen to break the monotony of the constraints the colour selection imposed. White with black polka dots, black with white polka dots, orange with white polka dots, white with orange polka dots, orange with black polka dots and black with orange polka dots. It was indeed a very dotty affair. This not only used dots in very creative ways, it also ignited the exploration of possibilities.

Removing constraints will also result in breakthroughs. A new CEO or change in legislation can create the opportunities that make something that previously could not be considered now part of the possibility mix. A new CEO may just support creativity and innovation and be so bold as to even declare it as a priority.

Most breakthroughs are combinations of ideas that already exist. The dingbat is the combination of a bat, a ball and a piece of elastic. The ability to spot trends and to recognise patterns creates a myriad of opportunities to form insights and to ignite breakthroughs.

Breakthroughs are more likely to happen in diverse teams. This sparked the trend in organisations to recruit and appoint people from different industries. The challenge is to then be able to engage these recruits in meaningful and value-adding roles. This proved to have been a challenge in some cases. The option to consider is for organisations not to hire these people but to invite them for a couple of days to come and trouble-shoot, challenge and question.

Breakthroughs are achieved by the creation of something new, and in our brains, it means the creation of new ideas, thoughts and new understandings. Having a new thought, any kind of new thought, requires the construction of a new connection inside our brains. How fast, how easily and how profusely we can create new connections greatly impacts how many breakthroughs we'll have. This can be the result of constantly being mindful of purposefully connecting seemingly un-connected things. The ability to create new connections inside our brain is known as neuroplasticity.

The higher our level of neuroplasticity, the higher our chances of breakthroughs. Children start developing their neuroplasticity from very early on and continually develop it as they start to connect information during the ever-present learning process. Then somehow, as adults, we regress from constantly exploring and engaging with everything around us, continually increasing our neuroplasticity, to being neural zombies. Our brains have gotten slack when it comes to creating new neural connections. When learning something new feels hard, we use age as an excuse sometimes stating that "we are too old for this kind of thing – it is for the younger minds". It's not that our brains are no longer capable of accumulating new information, but that we have not been keeping them in shape by developing our CQ on a regular basis. We need to actively engage in activities aimed at increasing the neuroplasticity of the brain. Engage in new experiences regularly.

The brain physically creates a new structure every time you experience or think about something new. It is this ability that enables us to have original thoughts and to create breakthroughs. Anything new you learn will promote your brain's plasticity. But ... learning something new while doing something physical doesn't just increase plasticity, it also increases the size of the neural circuit you are creating, which means – yeah, you have guessed it – more new connections. Plasticity increases when doing, learning and experiencing new things. The idea is to constantly gather as much information as you can. Even useless information may, when you least expect it, assist you to formulate that breakthrough idea.

Consciously engage with people who are different from you. Speak to people from different industries. Listen to other perspectives. Debate and argue. Study nature and find ways to apply what you see in a different context. Da Vinci as well as the Wright brothers studied the flight of birds to get ideas about what makes flight possible. This is referred to as biomimicking. Imagine a zebra with spots. The animal known as Marty in the movie *Madagascar* is a zebra, for those who are not familiar with what a zebra looks like. Alternatively, if you don't know what a zebra is or if you haven't seen *Madagascar*, picture a horse-like animal with black and white stripes. No orange though...definitely, no orange.

Take one small step at a time. One of the best tangible ways in which to ignite breakthroughs is to start by making notes. Please use a book – either this book or a brightly coloured notebook of your choice. Serviettes, Post-it notes, and tissues may not be such a good idea – they seem to somehow get lost and in this way so many a good idea has been lost to the world. If you do however get that paradigm-breaking moment of brilliance and you write or sketch your idea on the shower wall or glass, please make sure that you take a photo with your phone before the image disappears and the idea is lost forever.

Barriers that prevent us from being creative and killer phrases have been discussed earlier in this book. Some more information about idea crushers as promised earlier in the book follows.

Fox Cabane and Pollack aired the following views with regard to fear. Fear, whether it is the fear of making a mistake, the fear of being wrong or just the fear of your idea not being good enough, remains one of the greatest inhibitors of breakthrough ideas. It was found that negative thoughts and experiences ignite more neural activity than equally intense positive thoughts and experiences. We are unfortunately wired to more quickly recognise the negative in our world. Bad news sells more newspapers and results in higher reader ratings.

Fear of failure is real, and it is deeply rooted within our ancestral DNA. Both our own instincts and conventional wisdom seem to give us these two messages:

- Failure is bad. If you are failing, you are doing something wrong. If you do something wrong, you should be punished. Punishment is shameful, so you must avoid failures at all costs. Failure is shameful, and if you fail, you are a loser and the group will shun you.

- Failure is avoidable. If you're failing, you're doing something wrong. You should be able to avoid failure by doing everything right.

If you are not willing to risk failure, you won't innovate. Leaders and managers need to foster an environment and culture where risk-taking is encouraged and mistakes are viewed as learning experiences. All, of course, within the parameters of ethical and professional conduct.

Teams are often gathered to solve a specific and defined problem. A breakthrough is expected. The fear they may then experience is the fear of not being able to produce a breakthrough to solve that problem. The fear of failure can then in essence actually prevent them from suggesting all the possible things that they need to do in order to succeed. The team members may fear that the ideas they put forward may be considered too out-of-the-box or that it is impossible to implement the suggested ideas. This is what Fox Cabane and Pollock refer to as the focused-breakthrough-fear syndrome.

For unfocused or accidental breakthroughs, the fear comes after the breakthrough, but it is just as toxic as it is for focused breakthroughs. The accidental breakthrough may seem to come out of the blue – the result of a lengthy subconscious process. The expectation of a team having to reach a specific breakthrough in order to solve a problem, focused breakthroughs, raise the fear of not attaining a breakthrough, while unfocused or accidental breakthroughs raise the fear of not being able to implement the breakthrough.

Fear remains an integral part of the breakthrough process. The threat response impairs analytical thinking, creative insight, and problem solving. These crucial elements are essential in the process of unleashing your CQ. Social inhibition is essentially the fear of "what others would think". The fear of appearing stupid or being judged is the flip side of our social awareness. Social inhibitions are useful; it's the part of us that makes us "civilised", but it has its drawbacks.

Insights can only happen in the wake of quieting your frontal lobes, and that is where our inhibitions live. The problem with these inhibitions is that they can lead us to repress thoughts and ideas that could lead to breakthroughs. In some cases, diminished social inhibitions caused by the degeneration of the prefrontal lobes led people to a fountain of creativity – painting, art and so forth. People who had never had an artistic bone in their body suddenly became prolific artists. Fox Cabane and Pollack capture and embody the process of breakthrough thinking with the statement "Write drunk" but "Edit sober". Write drunk: drinking quiets the frontal lobes, the social inhibition part of our brain, the monitor. You quiet the EN and you let the DN run wild to generate a burst of breakthrough thinking. Edit sober; then you bring the EN back online to shift, evaluate and prioritise. This is the phase of convergent and critical thinking.

Common manifestations of the fear of failure are:

- The imposter syndrome: the fear that you will be exposed as a fraud
    - Solution: create a new self-image and support it with concrete evidence
- The inner critic: the voice in your head beating you up
    - Solution: find out what you mean when you tell yourself "everybody does this" then create a new "everybody" to think of instead
- The perfectionist: the feeling that you are never good enough, never doing enough
    - Solution: know that mistakes are precious and that others like your imperfections
- The maximiser: the drive to do better than everyone else, to do more.
    - Solution: place limits on how far you are willing to go

Fear is best handled with realisation, gratitude, self-forgiveness and self-compassion. Failure should be an opportunity to learn. Sometimes all you learn is "don't do that again". Change your vocabulary from "failure" to "gathering data" to improving the offering. A mindset like this will encourage you and others to experiment and to try again. The key is to view the journey of trial and error as a series of experiments on the way to a breakthrough.

Design a ceremony to get closure on a failure. Sometimes a debriefing session where you can list and discuss the lessons learnt is what is required. Maybe just write it down. Perhaps source something that represents the failure. Destroy it with gusto. Move on. Try and try again.

The fact is that no methodology, framework, technique or tool can guarantee breakthroughs, but they will assist your chances of success in getting there. If one approach does not work, try another. There is no harm in trying and who knows, you may just stumble onto that one great breakthrough by accident. Changing your mind is rewiring your mind. Every time you are changing your mind you are literally changing the response wiring in your brain. The neuroplasticity of your brain is being developed.

Guidelines on how to get the most out of the visualisation process:

- Rehearse it: Picture yourself doing what you need to do in order to achieve the desired outcome, rehearse it in your mind and do it as many times as necessary until you are satisfied with the result
- Rehearse in steps: Focus on the behaviours as you proceed through the process until you can successfully visualise the final outcome – you will know when you are ready for opening night
- Prepare for all possible scenarios: Imagine what could go wrong and be prepared

Uncertainty is not comfortable but it's a necessary step in achieving maximal creativity and achieving breakthroughs. Uncertainty can be balanced with healthy habits, rituals and routines in other areas of our lives. Start small when you want to form new habits or routines. Create incentives for yourself and don't beat yourself up when you fail. Fail fast, learn from it, move on. Start again should you wish to do so. Practise uncertainty in safe situations like re-writing movie scripts with several possible endings.

Fox Cabane and Pollock are of the opinion that a set of what they refer to as "super tools" ignite breakthroughs. These tools are a sense of higher purpose, aiming to achieve altruism by doing good and meditation. This resonates with the phases in the creative process. The higher purpose, that of turning your work into a mission, is the problem to be solved or the opportunity to be addressed. Altruism, the act of doing good, resonates with wanting to solve that problem or addressing the gap and meditation helps you relax the mind to set the scene for the Aha or Eureka moment to occur.

The following section will provide a brief overview of some breakthrough ideas that have changed the world. These breakthrough ideas are more often the result of revolutionary visionaries pushing to go where nobody has ever gone before. They dared to dream beyond the final frontiers of possibilities.

Science, invention and technology don't always take the straightest path and sometimes our greatest innovations have come in unexpected ways, through visionaries who were more revolutionary than evolutionary. The telescope – from Galileo to Hubble – allows humanity to reach the furthest limits of seeing – 13 billion light-years out.

From Leonardo da Vinci's flying machines to the Wright brothers who took to the sky to the modern commercial plane. One breakthrough idea and concept building on another. The ultimate freedom machine – the motor car. From Henry Ford's affordable and assembly-line-built Model T-Ford to scientists working on the next generation of self-driving automobiles. The rocket had its origin in a cave in ancient China, it then evolved to be used as a weapon of war and finally, by adding hydrogen, it was enabled to carry astronauts all the way to the moon. Then there is the fascinating history of the smartphone, from its roots in Morse Code to Alexander Graham Bell's invention of the telephone to Apple's 2007 unveiling of the first ever iPhone. The next generation smartphones will allow us to communicate through them by just thinking.[95]

Finally, robots were first conceptualised in ancient Rome and their use has evolved through the centuries from the calculator to the Roomba. We are currently living in a world where AI, VR, Robotics and 3D-printing are in the process of forever changing the world as we know it. We need to re-imagine, re-create and re-invent the world as we know it today. The 4IR requires us to navigate a world that is yet to be invented. It is always difficult to be part of a transition that will change the world beyond what has ever been portrayed in all the sci-fi and futuristic movies to date. *Star Trek, Star Wars, Passenger* – did we subconsciously create the worlds dictated to us by visionary imagineers in futuristic movies?

Reflections

- Breakthrough thinking is a skill you can acquire and practise

- Breakthrough thinking is the result of a process

- It is not a step-by-step process and it varies from individual to individual

- Fear inhibits breakthrough thinking

- Breakthrough in business is defined as an idea that solves a problem or satisfies a need

- There are two kinds of breakthroughs: focused breakthroughs and unfocused breakthroughs

- Breakthroughs are most likely to occur when you are no longer thinking about a problem

- Domain specialists achieve a level of mastery that opens the door to deep insights; do they just sometimes intuitively know whether or not something will work?

- The flipside is that specialisation can also inhibit breakthroughs and an outside perspective can help the specialist to view a domain from a different perspective and discover new possibilities

- Breakthroughs continue to baffle

Chapter 10

CQ(Creative Intelligence)@ Play...

What is possible when CQ is @ play?

Leonardo da Vinci is generally recognised as one of the great figures of the Renaissance and one of the greatest minds of all times. He was a thinker way ahead of his time and his inventions and ideas are prime examples of CQ@ Play personified.

Leonardo da Vinci changed the world in significant ways and it is a fitting introduction for subsequent examples of creativity and innovation in action. Leonardo da Vinci was a prolific note taker and the documents that survived show us his ideas for a wide range of devices. These documents include some of the first concepts of gliders, helicopters, parachutes, diving suits, cranes, gearboxes and many types of weapons of war. Many of these may be seen in use today, having taken the best part of 400 years to become practical realities.

He combined an imagination ahead of his time, an understanding of the emerging principles of science and engineering, and his superlative craftmanship to devise new uses for levers, gears, pulleys, bearings and springs. He despised war but was employed for much of this time as a military engineer. Leonardo's design of the 'tank' was flawed but many of his other inventions paved the way for some of today's weapons such as his design of ammunition which resembles today's 'cluster bombs'.

Da Vinci anticipated the idea of the helicopter, human-powered flying machines, used the mathematical principles of linear perspective to create the illusion of depth on a flat surface and his Vitruvian Man attempted to solve the problem of "squaring" a circle. It's not in fact possible to do this exactly (squaring a circle is a metaphor for the impossible), but he managed to come very close. He literally tried to put a square peg into a round hole.

Leonardo was not just fascinated by water's artistic features, he wanted to understand the fluid dynamics of water. Da Vinci made many contributions to modern water engineering and science including accurately describing the hydrological cycle, understanding the impact of flow speed on pressure, and engineering canals and reservoirs for flood management and irrigation. He is the driving force behind the foundations of water science and engineering.

Leonardo further developed the technique of creating "ambiguous" facial expressions where there is a constant "change" of appearance. Known as the technique of "sfumato", (from the Italian word for vanishing like smoke) where colours subtly change in hue to soften or obscure sharp edges, Da Vinci's use of this technique is unique and in many of his portraits it is almost impossible to say where one colour ends, and another starts.[96]

Let's now explore some more current examples of where good ideas have been successfully commercialised. The golden oldie: the glue that did not stick which resulted in the now most used creativity tool: Post-it notes. Milton was originally used as a water purifier but is now used as a general household steriliser, minimising odours and is also used to wash vegetables and fruit to prevent the spread of bacteria.[97]

As Patsy Sherman can attest, innovation is often triggered by unexpected and seemingly trivial occurrences. Hired by the 3M company as a chemist in 1952, Sherman became one of only a handful of female scientists in the field. She was assigned to work on fluorochemicals, where she and her colleague, Sam Smith, were charged with developing a new kind of rubber for jet aircraft fuel lines. An accidental spill in 1953 on a pair of white canvas tennis shoes led to an important discovery. They were fascinated to find that while the substance did not change the colour or the texture of the shoes, it could not be washed away by any solvents, and it repelled water, oil and other liquids. Sherman and Smith realised that they had stumbled onto an important discovery, one that could solve the problem of finding a commercially successful application for fluorochemical polymers. The research led to the development in 1956 of a versatile fabric stain repellent and material protector, Scotchgard. They explored the uses for the product and it eventually resulted in the development of the uses for the product to include a carpet treatment, automotive upholstery cleaner and numerous other derivations.[98]

The Hula Hoop is a round plastic circle that became a toy and exercise aid. The development of the virtual pet, the Tamagotchi, filled the need of people wanting something to nurture without having to look after an actual pet. And then there is the Pet Rock. Pet Rocks are smooth stones from Mexico's Rosarito Beach, and they were marketed like live pets, complete with straw and breathing holes. South Africans can order their Pet Rocks online from Takealot. The following business models changed the game completely by focusing on the customer need – Facebook, AirBnB, Uber, Bitcoin and Alibaba. NZ Air with their "cuddle class" seats for couples – three seats that fold into a bed. Drones used to deliver medicine and take-aways to customers. Embrace Infant Warmer which is a low-cost incubator saving the lives of many babies. The socks that inspire conversations: LittleMissMismatched.

BMW bought the British MINI Cooper, a brilliant 1959 design for a new small car that Alec Issigonis developed, and Jack Cooper improved in 1961. It is once again one of the world's top-selling city cars. This is an example of how the past can be mined by using what already exists and creatively adopting and re-framing it to suit the tastes of the current consumer.[99]

Creative applications of ideas have resulted in a vast number of innovations on the African continent. The founder of Apopo, Bart Weetjens, utilised and applied the incredible sense of smell of rats to detect landmines in countries such as Mozambique. Thousands of people die from tuberculosis every year but it can be treated and cured when detected early. Rats can detect tuberculosis in seven minutes while it takes a human one day in the lab to do so. Same set of skills and abilities applied in a different context for different purposes.

Access to safe water is one of the biggest global health challenges. Generally responsible for collecting water, women spend many hours doing so. They will often walk for miles carrying heavy pots, making the process potentially strenuous and unsafe. The inventors of the Hippo Water Roller project saw this problem and introduced the Hippo Water Roller as a solution. This is a round container fashioned with a handle so that it can be pushed. The roller requires much less effort to collect water, collects water more quickly and is able to carry more water per trip. This invention allows for more time and at the same time for more income-generating and education-related activities. This is another example of how a seemingly simple idea can change the lives of many.[100]

Now let's have a look at some of the top South African inventions of all times. *Time* magazine has listed the South African Wonderbag as one of its Top 50 genius products. The Wonderbag functions like a slow cooker, cooking food for up to twelve hours. Most of these bags are manufactured in Tongaat, KwaZulu-Natal. The idea came to Sarah Collins a decade ago while she was working in a community project in KwaZulu-Natal. She saw many households struggling to heat food amid the Eskom power crisis. The idea came to her when she woke up one morning remembering that her grandmother placed pots between cushions to keep the porridge warm by retaining the heat. This simple idea was utilised and the Wonderbag was born. Customised Wonderbags were given to Meghan Markle and Prince Harry as a wedding gift, courtesy of the Wonderbag team and the Lesotho royal family.[101]

Most people know that the first successful heart transplant was performed by Dr Chris Barnard, but do they know about other wonderful South African inventions such as the CAT scan, the Kreepy Krawly and Q20?

Let's now shift our focus closer to home and look in a little more detail as opposed to merely mentioning them, at some wonderful South African inventions. The CAT scan was developed by Cape Town physicist Allan Cormack and his associate Godfrey Hounsfield. He provided the mathematical technique for the CAT scan, in which an X-ray source and electronic detectors are rotated about the body and the resulting data are analysed by a computer to produce a sharp map of the tissue within a cross-section of the body. This resulted in a Nobel Prize in Physiology and Medicine.

South Africa had minimal oil reserves and the way in which the South African government addressed this need was to establish the South African Coal, Oil and Gas Corporation (Sasol). Sasol is the world's first – and largest – oil-from-coal refinery and it provides 40% of the country's fuel.

Dr Chris Barnard performed the world's first heart transplant in Cape Town on 3 December 1967. Dr Barnard took a chance and operated on Louis Washkansky, who was suffering heart failure. Dr Barnard became an international celebrity when the patient survived. Dr Barnard went on to perform more than ten other heart transplants with one of the recipients surviving a further 23 years.

The swimming pool vacuum cleaner was invented by Ferdinand Chauvier from Springs, a small town in South Africa. Chavier tried to figure out a way to take the hassle out of pool cleaning. The result was the Kreepy Krauly he created in 1974. Most pool owners in South Africa have been happy ever since.

The need for a type of glue that would hold components in an electrical box led to the invention of Pratley Putty. George Pratley's glue had a part in the success of the Moon Landing. In 1969, the substance was used to hold bits of Apollo11 mission's Eagle landing craft together. It is the only South African product to have ever gone to the moon.

Eric Merrifield created unusually shaped concrete blocks weighing up to 20 tons designed to break up wave action to protect harbour walls and coastal installations. These concrete structures are known as Dolosse. The Dolosse are used in almost every waterfront the world.

Q20 was invented in 1950 in Pinetown, KwaZulu-Natal by Mr Robertson. This product was required to displace water from distributor caps on the old VW Beetle, which was notorious for stalling in wet weather. It resulted in being an effective water repellent, kept rust at bay, eased squeaky door hinges and made it easy to release rusted or seized nuts and bolts. He battled to name the product. He mentioned to his neighbour that it certainly had 20 answers to 20 questions. Q20 is heavier than water and since oil floats on water, simply oiling the area will not resolve the problem. Q20 has a specific gravity which is heavier than the gravity of water. Q20 sinks to the bottom once it is sprayed on water where it acts as a water displacer and lubricant on the problem area. Up to Q20's invention, no such all-purpose product existed.

Dr Selig Percy Amoils, a specialist in retinal diseases, created a new method of cataract surgery at Baragwanath hospital in Soweto. The Amoils Cryo Pencil is the world's first surgical tool that uses extreme cold (nitrous oxide) to destroy unwanted tissue. It has been used to treat Margaret Thatcher's and Nelson Mandela's eyes. He achieved wide recognition for his invention and in 1975 received a Queen's Award for Technological Innovation. His cryoprobe has since been on display in the Kensington Museum in London.

The following invention could only come from a cricket-loving country. Henri Johnson invented the Speedball in 1992. The device accurately measures the speed and the angles of speeding objects such as a cricket and tennis balls.

Designers at South Africa's Vaal University of Technology developed the single-use syringes that protect against getting pricked by a used needle. Smartlock safety syringes provide improved protection against needlestick injury and contamination by Ebola virus, Hepatitis and HIV. This invention has saved countless lives.

Percy Trucker from Benoni (the same town where Charlize Theron grew up) transformed the events and entertainment industry in 1971 by developing the world's first computerised, centralised ticket-booking system – Computicket. Customers now don't have to stand in theatre queues for hours only to be informed that the cheapest and best tickets have already been sold out. Computicket soon secured Ster-Kinekor as its first client and the service took off in South Africa and internationally.

In 2005, University of Johannesburg physicist, Professor Vivian Alberts, developed solar power technology that uses a microthin metallic film instead of the much thicker and considerably more expensive silicon-based solar photovoltaic cells. This technology has made solar electricity in South Africa five times cheaper than the previous solar cells, giving people a more affordable energy source that's also great for the environment. And it's yet another reason why sunshine makes us happy.

A South African, Lesley Erica Scott, was recently awarded the Special Prize for Social Impact in Morocco this year for developing an effective calibration method for TB diagnostic machines. The latter are but a few fine examples of South Africa's creative potential and innovative prowess in action and at play. There are many more that can still be mentioned should the reader wish to explore further. South Africans are eager to pioneer and thankfully their ideas can further flourish in an investment climate that is considered the 12th most desirable for innovation in the world.

But[i] ...[102, 103, 104]

Besides recent innovative efforts, South Africa also boasts a history rich with intrepid inventors such as some of the examples mentioned before producing the likes of the Dolos, the CAT Scan, the speed gun, the Kreepy Krauly, the first heart transplant and Pratley Putty. The lesser known inventions such as SASOL and the Retinal Cryoprobe were also mentioned. Creativity and innovation in a South African context cannot be discussed without mentioning Mark Shuttleworth who gave the world the Ubuntu Linux operating system in 2004 and in 2008 Optima Energy gave us our very first, proudly South African, electric car – the Joule.

Recognising South Africa's innovative brilliance, a total of five Nobel Prizes have been bestowed upon South Africans in the fields of Chemistry, Physiology or Medicine. All five of these recipients have pushed the boundaries of innovation in their particular fields. A total of eleven Nobel Prizes have been claimed by South Africans over the years (the remaining six were for Peace or Literature). Enough to ensure that South Africa can claim to be the country with the 20th highest number of Nobel Laureates in the world – tied with Belgium and one more than Ireland.

It is indeed a reflection of the country's CQ@Play across fields and domains. But there is a catch and a challenge or two as there always is in South Africa. The majority of the Nobel Laureates and entrepreneurial and innovative greats such as Elon Musk (PayPal, Tesla Motors, SpaceX) and Mark Shuttleworth (Ubuntu Linux) have long since traded our beautiful country for the allure

---

i   The above information is a summary of the information obtained from the listed websites – endnotes 50-52.

of profit-maximising tax havens. In fact, according to the World Intellectual Property Organisation, only 1 of SA's top 15 entrepreneurs still lives in his/her country of birth.

You can shape, mould and offer environments conducive to innovation, but you can never force a driven individual, as these innovators most assuredly are, to stay when there are better opportunities abroad. This also holds true on more micro levels in an organisational context.

Reasons cited and speculations as to why so many are tempted to leave may be the fear for personal safety. Some articles speculate that it may be because South Africa is ranked only 61st in the ease of starting up a new business. It may also be that government spending on R&D is continually reduced. Will government's promise to double R&D investment by 2019 be enough to keep our keen minds where they are most needed – here at home?

One thing is for certain. South Africa as a country can still proudly hold its own in the halls of international innovation. We are a nation that has proven again and again that we boast creative minds and innovative potential sufficient to compete internationally with the best of the best. But for how long will our CQ still be @ play despite the financial and legislative support for innovation, if we cannot stem the tide of brilliant, passionate and creative South African minds leaving. Brain drain is a reality – even the drive to lure some of those brilliant minds back to the country did not result in the return of the much-needed intellectual capital our country so desperately needs. Will we lose our right to maintain our place in those halls or will we embrace our creative and innovative minds and thrive against the odds? This is after all South Africa, a country that has on many occasions surprised the world at what we are capable of.

After all, anything is possible when a nation consciously puts its collective CQ@Play to unleash the inner Barnards, Amoils, Van Aardts, Musks, Shuttleworths, and Ibrahims to design a future fitting to be showcased on a world stage.

 # Reflections

- Leonardo da Vinci is recognised as one of the greatest minds of all times

- Da Vinci was a thinker way ahead of his time and his ideas personified CQ@Play imagining and creating future "What if's..."

- It has taken the best part of 400 years for some of his ideas to become practical realities

- Innovations are often triggered by unexpected and sometimes seemingly trivial occurrences e.g. Scotchgard

- Some ideas fill needs (virtual pet) while others are industry game changers e.g. Uber and AirBnB

- Creative applications of ideas have resulted in a vast number of creative applications in Africa, e.g. Hippo Roller, Wonderbag and Infant Warmer

- More focus and recognition should be given to proudly South African CQ@Play

- A conscious effort should be made to retain South Africa's CQ locally, celebrating and utilising the achievements of our innovators and game changers, while showcasing their brilliance on global stages

Creativity gives us the ability to see things in a different way, and the courage to step out and do something in a way that hasn't been done before.

Jane Chu

Chapter 11

Reflections...

So where does this leave us?

We are on the verge of what the World Economic Forum refers to as the 4IR (Fourth Industrial Revolution). Artificial intelligence, automation, mobile supercomputing, intelligent robots, self-driving cars, neuro-technological brain enhancements, genetic editing are all elements hovering on the cusp of a revolution that is going to change the world and everything as we know it in ways not yet imagined. The evidence of dramatic change is all around us and it is happening at exponential speed.

This new revolution brings exciting opportunities, new solutions to global challenges and employment opportunities for jobs that have yet to be invented. Governments, industries, educators, trainers and the entire global community must co-create a solution to how to prepare present and future generations to thrive in this rapidly transforming world.

The value-add will be to mine the past, connect the dots and to understand what people find meaningful. Find your orange unicorn. What is your differentiator? Make innovation a game. Play and have fun. Capitalise on what makes each generation tick. Build business models around the values and needs of specific generations. Be willing to partner with people whose insider knowledge exceeds your own. There is a gap in the assumption that Boomers will never get what their kids and grandkids understand about the latest technology and culture that comes with that technology. Boomers will not be as skilled in using the new tools as the current generation is. But Boomers will be selective users of these tools to satisfy their unique needs. A grandmother learning to use WhatsApp in order to stay connected with all the generations in her tribe spanning across generations, the Boomer generation satisfying their need to showcase their lust for life on Facebook and trainers becoming familiar with training virtually utilising tools such as Zoom, BlueJeans and Skype. The current generation will obviously use technology differently. And so it should be. They have grown up with computers as their main form of communication and learning. The key is to cultivate awareness about the skills, knowledge and beliefs and learn to engage and understand the new audiences.

 Access the embodied knowledge of all the generations. What is the value-add of each generation? Look at the "What is" and the "What if". We do not always have to create something out of nothing. We can start with what already exists. Artists, dancers and writers have long known the importance of mining the past. Look at something and instead of copying it, translate it into something else.

Despite the first signs of a massive shift about to take place, most schools still teach in the same old way. Learners still have to memorise chunks of dated curriculum and the grading still mostly relies on merely reproducing information. The entire character of the learner and different learning needs and styles are still not taken into consideration.

The reality is that jobs of the future will be the ones that machines can't do, and it is fair to state that anything that can be measured or is based on rules will be automated. This is great news because it means that **we can automate the jobs and humanise the work.**

Humans still have the competitive edge when it comes to areas such as:

- **Creative endeavours:** anything ranging from scientific discovery, creative writing and entrepreneurship

- **Social interaction:** robots just don't have the kind of emotional intelligence that humans do

- **Physical dexterity and mobility:** millennia of hiking mountains, swimming lakes and dancing practice give humans extraordinary agility and dexterity

So how then does one sell these breakthrough ideas and innovative products? Don't sell a product or a service, sell a new way of thinking. Pilot customers and early adopters are usually enthusiastic but, in most cases, broader adoption is slow even with customer support and training. Information, data and value propositions are not enough to sell innovative products. Potential supporters will not see the benefits without the right mental model. In order to change an existing mental model, one first needs to shift the thinking and then the behaviour.

Present the model of how things work today. If you are trying to get people to see a problem or opportunity, focus on disrupting their existing mental model. Then provide them with a model of how things could be in the future. If you are trying to get people to understand the benefits of your solution, focus on shifting their thinking in a way that reveals why your solution would be effective. Do people recognise the problem, and the value of your solution, but fail to make the change? Define a roadmap that explains to them how to get from where they are to where they want to go. Then build the programme. People need to see how the new way of thinking plays out in different contexts and situations.[105]

People who are routinely creative put their CQ to play and they become skilled at connecting information from various sources in new and surprising ways. They know how to mine for new ideas – combining information from different fields and disciplines or how to revisit old ideas from the past and how they can be applied in different contexts. Fortunate are those people with such deep domains of knowledge and expertise who can intuitively spot opportunities and identify gaps.

What we need, perhaps more than ever, are individuals and organisations who are not cut off from but are rather intimately connected to the world around them.

For many people it goes like this: Get up from the same side of the bed you always sleep on (with your bedtime reading conveniently piled next to you), drive the same route to work, go to your favourite coffee shop, chat to the same barista you see every day, whilst waiting for your regular morning coffee. But, once in the office, you have to navigate around to find a free space in the hot desk area, retrieve your books and papers from an inconveniently located locker, interact politely with people sitting nearby that you barely know and set up your workstation so it's how you like it. Spot the difference? Change is good. New people are interesting. But... making additional choices and building relationships deplete energy and decision-making capacity. That's why people like routine and certainty – it allows mental energy and CQ to be focused where it is needed. Modern, open-plan, activity-based workplace design doesn't fit with how people choose to live most of their actual lives. Why? Because it's often cost reduction dressed up as good practice, rather than genuine good practice built for humans.

So, what do we need to be competent in the world today? Kelley & Kelley[106] are of the opinion that you need two abilities to be competent in the world today. You need analytical ability and the tools that go with it and you need creative ability and the tools that go with it. You need to partner with people whose insider knowledge exceeds your own. Constantly learn new things. Combine computer science with art and design. Mine the past for inspiration. Spend time thinking about how to connect with what people find meaningful. You need to develop Design Intelligence and Creative Intelligence and you need the confidence to put these intelligences to play. The idea is to make the practice of creativity routine.

So, what does this all mean? The challenge still remains: How do we navigate the challenges of the 4IR in a VUCA world where rapid, exponential change is the only constant? CQ@Play!

A FINAL WORD OR TWO...

- The 4IR is going to change the world and everything we know in ways not yet imagined

- Change is the only constant and it is happening @an exponential speed

- The entire global community must co-create a solution to how to prepare present and future generations to thrive in this rapidly transforming world

- Each generation will hopefully utilise technology and other trends to suit their specific needs

- The way we learn needs to change

- The entire character of the learner, as well as different learning needs and styles, need to be re-imagined

- Jobs and value-add need to be re-imagined

- There are things that humans can do that machines still cannot do – capitalise on that

- Innovators change the lens through which we see the world

- Sell a new way of thinking

- Fast-track broader adoption of ideas and new ways of doing

- Companies that successfully market and sell innovation are able to shift how people think not only about their product, but also about themselves, the market and the world

- Routine allows you to focus on that which truly matters – your job and CQ@Play

- Innovation is creativity in a business suit

CREATIVITY SMORGASBORD...
Fifty thrifty thoughts about creativity...

1. The creative must follow the road less travelled or even, at times, build the road as he/she travels it

2. Doing something new for the first time is always daunting – it gets better the more you do it and it develops and increases the neuroplasticity of the brain

3. Practise, practise and practise some more – re-frame failures and mistakes as learning opportunities

4. Something needs to be done 21 times or for 21 days to establish a habit or to break a habit

5. Creativity is the fragrance of individual freedom

6. Celebrate the weird ones

7. Celebrate and embrace the C-sweet: consciousness, compassion, change, collaboration, communication and CREATIVITY

8. Creativity ignites ideas which require ACTION – an idea not implemented is just an idea

9. If you can imagine it, you can make it happen – your imagination becomes your reality

10. The real artist thinks of totality – never of perfection

11. Creativity means bringing the new into existence, paving the way for the unknown – turning the unknown into the known

12. The creative does something that nobody has ever done before

13. Think what nobody else is thinking

14. See what nobody else is seeing

15. Look at things from different perspectives

16. Make your thoughts visible: draw, build a prototype, mind-mapping, idea plotting

17. Look for opportunities

18. Look at the problem/challenge/task in a different way – phrase it differently

19. Look for a new point of view

20. Ask the right questions

21. Think like a child – access your inner child or talk to children

22. The creative is always ready to take a risk

23. Creative means the new, the novel, the original

24. Be a dreamer, as well as a doer

25. Life is an opportunity to create meaning

26. Combine domains, clusters, talents, ideas and constantly revise them

27. Connect the seemingly unconnected

28. Meaning comes out of creativity

29. Do a couple of crazy things, then meaning will be possible!

30. Are you crazy enough?

31. Imagine

32. Use metaphors

33. Consciously become more creative in your work and in your personal life

34. Allow for enough time to incubate

35. Build a creative network

36. Creativity is a team sport – you don't have to generate all the ideas yourself or on your own

37. Turn creativity into a habit

38. Daydream – let the mind wonder

39. Disrupting yourself is the secret to breaking into a new field, never settling for less, and achieving more.

40. Remember the importance of the role that reflecting, processing and not doing play in creativity

41. The outcome of any creative endeavour must produce something that is meaningful

42. Translate insights into a compelling narrative or story

43. There is a shift from an economy that valued things to an economy that valued experiences

44. Learn to navigate the uncertainty within

45. Re-frame failure as an opportunity to learn

46. Constantly explore to find and discover new sources of information and learning

47. Creativity is required to not only build a world-class design capability, but to also make a significant difference in society

48. Creativity and innovation are more than just satisfying needs – create an understanding of what people find meaningful

49. A combination of triggers, tools and trends are required to imagine the unimaginable to establish and shift the required behaviour

50. "Creativity is intelligence having fun!" Albert Einstein

INTENTIONS...

What pearls of wisdom should you take from this book?

- Everyone is creative and creativity can be developed

- You need to decide to be creative and consciously develop your creative confidence

- Start by keeping notes and by doing as little as one creativity exercise a day

- Don't play by the rules (but remain ethical!)

- You owe it to yourself to re-discover, re-capture and re-channel your inherent creative potential

- You are more creative than you think – you need to discover what you don't know you know and what you already have – the gift to imagine

- Address and overcome your fear of failure – then creativity becomes a lot easier

- View failure as an opportunity to learn

- Draw your ideas – a picture paints 1 000 words

- If you are required to be creative in solving a client problem, start by identifying their needs and by having empathy for their situation

- Always have a prototype ready

- The culture must be supportive of creativity and innovation – if it is not, create and establish a culture supportive of creativity and innovation

- People at every level need to understand how to influence culture and cultivate change

- Grow the creative confidence of your organisation, create a culture of innovation

- And if all else fails develop and enhance your CQ by…

  - Using good old fashioned mind-maps or even electronic versions should you be so inclined

  - Taking notes – lots of notes

  - Doing the triangle exercise on a regular basis

  - Thinking the opposite

  - Constantly re-inventing yourself

  - Reading as much as possible about as many topics as possible – lifelong-learning

  - Collaborating and connecting the dots

  - Making mistakes – learning from them

  - Never giving up – try & try, again & again!

- MOST IMPORTANT OF ALL – GIVE YOUR CQ PERMISSION TO PLAY!

EPILOGUE

"Success is not final, failure is not fatal, it is the courage to continue that counts".
—Sir Winston Churchill, Former British Prime Minister[107]

Much food for thought has been provided in the preceding pages. Each chapter ends with a summary of significant insights and the book itself concludes with essential bullet points that the reader can take with him or her as they proceed along a path of greater awareness of the many facets of crucial challenges posed by creativity and innovation in our daily lives.

Those of us who were born in the previous century have experienced first-hand the momentous changes that have taken place that have both enhanced, but also made our reality more complex. I suppose if one is forced to choose, we would probably consider developments in medicine, communication technology and travel as those that have had the most profound impact. Who can miss or ignore the powerful role that social media now play throughout the world? It all does however underline for us the inevitability of change, and perhaps more disconcerting and challenging, the ever-increasing pace of change that we need to adapt to. The certainty of change, and in particular of technological change, associated with the 4th Industrial Revolution and its consequences for the world of work cannot be underestimated. This book has made clear that the world of work will change. The knowledge, and hard and soft skills that will provide entry to the labour market and ensure survival will change and, all indications are, that the sophistication of the knowledge and skills will rise. Once-off training will become a bygone phenomenon to be replaced by continuous training and updating by means of formal education institutions and on-the-job training provided by corporations, industry and government services. Formal employment opportunities could shrink, though rather fortunately the changes anticipated will also create new job opportunities, many of which we are not yet able to anticipate. Good basic skills (language facility, numeracy skills and social skills) will enhance our ability to respond to change. At the same time, entrepreneurial skills will be in great demand, particularly where formal employment opportunities become scarcer. In all these endeavours the significance of creativity and innovation is immediately apparent. The emphasis in this book on innovation as creativity made productive and marketable, is the note on which I would like to conclude. In his book *The New Alchemists* Charles Handy[108] reflects the interviews he did with some 27 international entrepreneurs, some extremely well-known. The one very striking thing that emerges from the book is the number of times many of the entrepreneurs failed in their businesses before they ultimately found the right niche and business that became very profitable and successful and that solidified their considerable reputations. This phenomenon reveals at least two truths, that (1) innovation is not for the faint-hearted and (2) that persistence and mental toughness to find the right opportunity will be required to succeed.

Finally, and in the light of the above, another quote by Sir Winston Churchill may be appropriate (and encouraging!!):

"Continuous effort – not strength or intelligence – is the key to unlocking our potential"[109]

ENDNOTES

1. Toffler, A. (1970). *Future Shock*. New York: Random House.
2. Karodia, Y. (2019). *#BixTrends2019: Top 11 trends in South African education*. Retrieved from: https://www.bizcommunity.com/Article/196/722/185945.html
3. Deloitte. (2018). Preparing tomorrow's workforce for the Fourth Industrial Revolution: For business: A framework for action. Retrieved from: https://www2.deloitte.com/content/dam/Deloitte/global/Documents/About-Deloitte/gx-preparing-tomorrow-workforce-for-4IR.pdf
4. Nussbaum, B. (2013). *Creative Intelligence: Harnessing the Power to Create, Connect, and Inspire*. New York: HarperCollins Publishers.
5. Ibid.
6. Nussbaum, B. (2013). *Creative Intelligence: Harnessing the Power to Create, Connect, and Inspire*. New York: HarperCollins Publishers.
7. Toffler, A. (1970). *Future Shock*. New York: Random House.
8. Karodia, Y. (2019). #Biz Trends 2019: Top 11 trends in South African education. Retrieved from: https://www.bizcommunity.com/Article/196/722/185945.html
9. It's Nice That. (2017). Serpentine appoints Francis Kéré to build "tree-inspired" 2017 pavilion. Retrieved from: https://www.itsnicethat.com/articles/francis-kere-serpentine-pavilion-210217
10. iAfrica. (2019). Five Ways Businesses Can Take Advantage of Industry 4.0. Retrieved from: https://www.iafrica.com/five-ways-businesses-can-take-advantage-of-industry-4-0/
11. Pedro, L. (2018). 5 African Trends for 2018. Retrieved from: https://trendwatching.com/quarterly/2017-11/5-african-trends-2018/
12. De Jager, C. (2010). *The development of creative and innovative thinking and problem-solving skills in a financial services organization*. Published doctoral dissertation. University of Johannesburg, Johannesburg, South Africa.
13. Baumgartner. J. (2019). Ten Steps for Boosting Creativity. Retrieved from: https://www.creativejeffrey.com/creative/creative.php
14. Wiseman, L. (2012). Introduction to Multipliers. The Growth Faculty. Retrieved from: https://www.youtube.com/watch?v=Wmk8bhKJbfM
15. Gallo, P. & Hlupic, V. (2019). Humane leadership must be the Fourth Industrial Revolution's real innovation. Retrieved from: https://www.weforum.org/agenda/2019/05/humane-leadership-is-the-4irs-big-management-innovation/
16. Ibid.
17. Nussbaum, B. (2013). *Creative Intelligence: Harnessing the Power to Create, Connect, and Inspire*. New York: HarperCollins.
18. Kelley, T. & Kelley, D. (2015). *Creative Confidence: Unleashing the creative potential in us all*. London, UK: HarperCollins, 202-203
19. Krippendorff, K. (2008). *The way of innovation*. Avon, Massachusetts: Platinum Press.
20. Gardner, H. (n.d.). Howard Gardner Multiple Intelligences. Retrieved from: https://video.search.yahoo.com/yhs/search;_ylt=AwrEZ66A2lhcv3IA_ewPxQt.;_ylu=X3oDMTByMDgyYjJiBGNvbG8DYmYxBHBvcwMyBHZ0aWQDBHNlYwNzYw--?p=howard+gardner+multiple+intelligences&fr=yhs-avg-fh_lsonswrow&hspart=avg&hsimp=yhs-fh_lsonswrow

21 Gardner, H. (1982). *Art, mind and brain*. New York: Basic Books.
22 Rowe, A.J. (2004). *Creative intelligence: Discovering the innovative potential in ourselves and others*. New York: Pearson, Prentice Hall.
23 Møller, C. (2005). Creative Intelligence Executive Summary. Retrieved from: http://www.openwindows.se/ow2/doc/Claus_M/Creative_Intelligence-CMC%5B1%5D.pdf
24 Carman, S. (2017). Three basic principles of creative intelligence. Retrieved from: https://www.enliveningedge.org/columns/three-basic-principles-creative-intelligence/
25 Nussbaum, B. (2013). *Creative Intelligence: Harnessing the Power to Create, Connect, and Inspire*. New York: HarperCollins Publishers.
26 Ibid.
27 Møller, C. (2005). Creative Intelligence Executive Summary. Retrieved from: http://www.openwindows.se/ow2/doc/Claus_M/Creative_Intelligence-CMC%5B1%5D.pdf
28 Crimson. (2017). Top 10 Jobs in 2030: Skills you need now to land the jobs of the future. Retrieved from: https://www.crimsoneducation.org/za/blog/jobs-of-the-future
29 Beckford, A. (2018). The Skills You Need to Succeed in 2020. Retrieved from: https://www.forbes.com/sites/ellevate/2018/08/06/the-skills-you-need-to-succeed-in-2020/#1576a9ba288a
30 Amabile, T.M. (1983). *The social psychology of creativity*. New York: Springer-Verlag.
31 Amabile, T.M. (1989). *Growing up creative*. Buffalo, New York: C.E.F. Press.
32 Amabile, T.M. (2003). *Motivation in software communities: Work environment support*. Seminar held at the Harvard Business School, Boston, Massachusetts.
33 Guilford, J.P. (1975). Creativity: A quarter century of progress. In I.A. Taylor & J.W. Getzels, (Eds.). *Perspectives in creativity*. 37-59. Chicago: Aldine Publishing Co.
34 Guilford, J.P. (1986). *Creative talents: Their nature, uses, and development*. New York: Barely Limited.
35 Barron, F. (1969). *Creative person and creative process*. New York: Holt, Rinehart and Winston, Inc.
36 Barron, F. (1990). *Creativity and psychological health: Origins of personal vitality and creative freedom*. Buffalo, NY: Creative Education Foundation.
37 Tannenbaum, A. (1997). *Creativity boosters: An exploration of possibilities*. Proceedings from the International Association of Facilitators Conference, Tulsa, OK.
38 West, M.A. & Farr, J.L. (1990). Innovation at work: psychological perspectives. *Social Behavior*, 4: 15-30.
39 Burkus, D. (2014). *The Myths of Creativity*. San Francisco: Jossey Bass.
40 Burkus, D. (n.d.). The Myths of Creativity: An Interview with David Burkus. Retrieved from: https://video.search.yahoo.com/yhs/search?fr=yhs-avg-fh_lsonswrow&hsimp=yhs-fh_lsonswrow&hspart=avg&p=david+burkus+the+myths+of+creativity+youtube#id=5&vid=7e8d3b3ed130409b7c73d527c5cc46e0&action=click
41 Black, R.A. (1990). *Cre8ing People, Places & Possibilities*. Athens, Georgia: RAB Inc.
42 Black, R.A. (1990). *Cre8ing People, Places & Possibilities*. Athens, Georgia: RAB Inc.
43 Perkins, D.N. (1984). Creativity by design. *Educational Leadership*, Sept: 18-25.
44 Perkins Rodriquez, S. (2002). *What is really driving performance? The impact of enabling creativity and innovation within the organisation*. New York University: Stern School of Business.
45 Spranger, O. (1928). Lebensformen. In Jordaan, J. & Jordaan, W. (1998). *People in Context*. Sandton: Heinemann.

46	De Jager, C. (2010). *The development of creative and innovative thinking and problem-solving skills in a financial services organization*. Published doctoral dissertation. University of Johannesburg, Johannesburg, South Africa.
47	Nussbaum, B. (2013). *The Search for the Secrets of Creativity, Creative Intelligence*, New York: HarperCollins.
48	Betsy, Ng. & Ong A.K.K. (2018). Neuroscience and Digital Learning Environments in Universities: What does current research tells us? *Journal of the Scholarship of Teaching and Learning*, 18(3): 116-131.
49	Leighton, J. (2017). Using neuroscience tools that develop creative skills that sells. *International Journal of Market Research*, 59(6): 1-6.
50	Solikan, M.J. & Farid, A. (2018). Transformation Leadership through applied neuroscience: Transmission Mechanism of the Thinking Process. *International Journal of Organizational Leadership*, 7: 211-229.
51	Quote Investigator. (2012). Thomas Edison Quote. Retrieved from: https://quoteinvestigator.com/2012/12/14/genius-ratio/
52	Guilford, J.P. (1986). *Creative talents: Their nature, uses, and development*. New York: Barely Limited.
53	Barron, F. (1969). *Creative person and creative process*. New York: Holt, Rinehart and Winston, Inc.
54	Gelb, M. (1998). *How to think like Leonardo Da Vinci: seven steps to genius every day*. New York, N.Y.: Delacorte Press.
55	Gelb, M. (n.d.). How to Think Like Leonardo Da Vinci! Seven Steps to Genius Every Day! Retrieved from: https://video.search.yahoo.com/yhs/search?fr=yhs-avg-fh_lsonswrow&hsimp=yhs-fh_lsonswrow&hspart=avg&p=how+to+think+like+leonardo+da+vinci#id=1&vid=415c7609049391e70690f6cc6a929197&action=view
56	Guilford, J.P. (1986). *Creative talents: Their nature, uses, and development*. New York: Barely Limited.
57	Barron, F. (1969). *Creative person and creative process*. New York: Holt, Rinehart and Winston, Inc.
58	Guilford, J.P. (1986). *Creative talents: Their nature, uses, and development*. New York: Barely Limited.
59	De Bono, E. (1995). *Parallel thinking: From Socratic Thinking to De Bono Thinking*. London: Penguin Books.
60	De Bono, E. (1992). *Serious creativity: Using the Power of Lateral Thinking to Create New Ideas*. New York: Harper Collins Publishers.
61	Barron, F. (1969). *Creative person and creative process*. New York: Holt, Rinehart and Winston, Inc.
62	Kelley, T. & Kelley. D. (2014). *Creative Confidence: Unleashing the Creative Potential within Us All*. Harper Collins: London. 61.
63	Levesque, L.C. (2001*). Breakthrough Creativity: Achieving Top Performance Using the Eight Creative Talents*. Palo Alto, CA: Davies Black Publishing.
64	VanGundy, A.B. (1990). Solutions to all your problem-solving retreats. *Training and Development Journal*, 44(2): 18-20.
65	Von Oech, R. (1990). *A whack on the side of the head: How you can be more creative*. London: Thorsons.
66	Von Oetinger, B. (2004). From idea to innovation: Making creativity real. *Journal of Business Strategy*, 25(5): 35-41.

67 Idea Sandbox. (n.d.). Osborn: Creative Problem-Solving Process. Retrieved from: https://idea-sandbox.com/destination/osborn-creative-problem-solving-process/#axzz5zh0bAHol
68 De Jager, C (2010). *The development of creative and innovative thinking and problem-solving skills in a financial services organization*. Published doctoral dissertation. University of Johannesburg, Johannesburg, South Africa.
69 McFadzean, E. (1998). Enhancing creative thinking within organisations. *Management Decision*, 36(5): 309-315.
70 VanGundy, A.B. (1987). Idea collection methods: Blending old and new technology. *Journal of Data Collection*, 27(1): 14-19.
71 VanGundy, A.B. (1990). Solutions to all your problem-solving retreats. *Training and Development Journal*, 44(2): 18-20.
72 VanGundy, A.B. (1992). *Idea power: Techniques to unleash the creativity in your organisation*. New York: AMACOM.
73 VanGundy, A.B. (1997). "I.D.E.A.S. for ideal brainstorming." Proceedings from the International Association of Facilitators Conference, Tulsa, OK.
74 Baumgartner, J. (2013). Creativity & Beer: Brainstorming & Anticonventional Thinking (ACT). Retrieved from: https://youtu.be/TROI8xPVKu8
75 De Jager, C., Muller, A., Roodt, G. (2013). Developing Creative and Innovative Thinking and Problem-Solving Skills in a Financial Services Organisation. Retrieved from: https://www.questia.com/library/journal/1P3-3117255721/developing-creative-and-innovative-thinking-and-problem-solving
76 Baumgartner, J. (2019). *Ten Steps for Boosting Creativity*. Retrieved from: https://www.creativejeffrey.com/creative/creative.php
77 Idea Sandbox. (n.d.). Osborn: Creative Problem-Solving Process. Retrieved from: https://idea-sandbox.com/destination/osborn-creative-problem-solving-process/#axzz5zh0bAHol
78 Nussbaum, B. (2013). *Creative Intelligence*. HarperCollins Publishers: New York.
79 Von Oech, R. (1983). *A whack on the side of the head: How you can be more creative*. New York: Warner Brothers Inc.
80 Von Oech, R. (1990). *A whack on the side of the head: How you can be more creative*. London: Thorsons.
81 Von Oech, Roger. (2008). *A whack on the side of the head: How you can be more creative*. New York: Little, Brown & Company.
82 De Bono, E. (1992). *Serious creativity: Using the Power of Lateral Thinking to Create New Ideas*. New York: Harper Collins Publishers.
83 De Bono, E. (1995). *Parallel thinking: From Socratic Thinking to De Bono Thinking*. London: Penguin Books.
84 Dam, R.F. & Teo, Y.S. (2017). Learn How to Use the Best Ideation Methods: SCAMPER. Retrieved from: https://www.interaction-design.org/literature/article/learn-how-to-use-the-best-ideation-methods-scamper
85 Wikipedia. (2020). S.C.A.M.P.E.R. Retrieved from: https://en.wikipedia.org/wiki/S.C.A.M.P.E.R
86 Medium.com. (2015). Thinking the Opposite is an Extraordinary Way to Get Creative. Retrieved from: https://medium.com/productivity-revolution/thinking-the-opposite-is-an-extraordinary-way-to-get-creative-692009120a24

87 Board of Innovation. (n.d.). Opposite thinking. Retrieved from: https://www.boardofinnovation.com/tools/opposite-thinking/
88 Liedtka, J. & Ogilvie, T. (2011) *Designing for Growth: a design thinking toolkit for managers*. Columbia University Press: New York.
89 Kimbell, L. (2011). Rethinking Design Thinking: Part 1. *Design and Culture*, 3(3): 285-301.
90 Johansson-Sköldberg, U., Woodilla, J. & Cetinkaya, M. (2013). *Design Thinking: Past, Present and Possible futures*. John Wiley and Sons Ltd., 22(2): 121-146.
91 Martin, R. (2010). Design thinking: achieving insights via the "knowledge funnel". The Design of Business: Why Design Thinking is the Next Competitive Advantage. 38(2): 37-42.
92 Fox Cabane, O. & Pollack, J. (2017). *The Net and The Butterfly*. New York: Penguin Random House.
93 Ibid.
94 Ibid.
95 PBS. (2019). PBS Takes Viewers on a Mind-Blowing Journey Through History with New Series BREAKTHROUGH: THE IDEAS THAT CHANGED THE WORLD. Retrieved from: https://www.pbs.org/about/blogs/news/pbs-takes-viewers-on-a-mind-blowing-journey-through-history-with-new-series-breakthrough-the-ideas-that-changed-the-world/
96 World Economic Forum. (2019). Here are 4 significant ways that Leonardo da Vinci changed the world. Retrieved from: https://www.weforum.org/agenda/2019/05/four-ways-in-which-leonardo-da-vinci-was-ahead-of-his-time
97 Google search. (n.d.). Uses for Milton sterilizing fluid. Retrieved from: https://www.google.co.za/search?source=hp&ei=Hb7RXP2DH82bkwXZy7HgCg&q=uses+for+milton+sterilising+fluid&oq=uses+for+milton+ster&gs_l=mobile-gws-wiz-hp.1.0.0j33i-21j33i160.3018.16610..18789...6.0..0.447.7391.2-14j9j2......0....1.......8..41j0i131j46j33i22i29i30j0i22i30..3%3A1.nLYU5Fil4Sl
98 Famous Women Inventors. (2008). Patsy Sherman: Invention of Scotchgard™ Stain Repellent. Retrieved from: http://www.women-inventors.com/Patsy-Sherman.asp
99 Storm12. (2018). Design Classics – The Mini. Retrieved from: https://www.storm12.co.uk/blog/design/design-classics-the-mini/
100 Coughlan, C. (2015). African innovations that can change the world. Retrieved from: https://www.one.org/international/blog/surprising-innovations-that-are-changing-the-world/
101 Cabox, J. (2018). *Time* magazine has named this South African invention one of its top 50 'genius' products. Retrieved from: https://www.businessinsider.co.za/time-magazine-has-named-this-south-african-invention-one-of-its-top-50-genius-products-worldwide-2018-10
102 Global South Africans Network. (2019). Top 10 South African inventions. Retrieved from: https://www.sagoodnews.co.za/top-10-south-african-inventions/
103 First Car Rental. (2019). 10 World-First Innovations you probably didn't know were invented by South Africans. Retrieved from: https://www.firstcarrental.co.za/news/travel/10-great-south-african-inventions.html
104 Louw, N. R. (2015). Top 20 South African innovations of all time [infographic]. Retrieved from: https://www.thesouthafrican.com/opinion/top-20-south-african-innovations-of-all-time-infographic/

105 Bonchek, M. (2014). Don't Sell a Product, Sell a Whole New Way of Thinking. Retrieved from: https://hbr.org/2014/07/dont-sell-a-product-sell-a-whole-new-way-of-thinking
106 Kelley, T. & Kelley, D. (2015). *Creative Confidence: Unleashing the creative potential in us all*. London, UK: HarperCollins.
107 BrainyQuote. (n.d.). Winston Churchill quotes. Retrieved from: https://www.brainyquote.com/quotes/winston_churchill_124653
108 Handy, C. (1999). *The New Alchemists*. London: Hutchinson Press.
109 BrainyQuote. (n.d.). Winston Churchill quotes. Retrieved from: https://www.brainyquote.com/quotes/liane_cordes_385862

INDEX

A

ability, 6–10, 18, 30, 39–40, 43, 45, 61, 63–64, 67, 121–122, 131, 142, 149
  analytical, 142
  developing, 8
  extraordinary, 61
accountabilities, 23, 34
  social, 34
action learning strategies, 66
action orientation, 23
actions, 22, 31–32, 44, 51, 70, 73, 80, 89, 91, 106, 108, 116, 120, 129, 135
  creative, 116
  cultural, 36
  innovative, 33
active learning, 6
activity-based workplace design, 142
agenda of ideas, 60
Albert Einstein, 108, 146
ambidexterity, 82
analogical relationships, 64
analogies, 39, 61, 119
analytical thinking, 124
  strong, 6
ancestral DNA, 123
ancient China, 127
ancient Rome, 127
application of CQ, 37, 61, 77
application of creativity, 90
archaic concept, 46
archaic pedagogic practices, 5
art and creativity, 21
artificial intelligence, 1, 12, 47, 63, 139

B

Baby Boomers, 47
balance, between empowerment and guidance 34
  lifestyle, 14
balance between analytical mastery, intuitive originality and creativity, 110
basic principles of CQ, 43
BDNF (brain-derived-neurotropic factor), 120
biomimicking, 40, 123
blended learning options, 16
blended methodologies, 47
blocks to creativity, 57, 91
body language, 40
Body-Kinaesthetic Intelligence, 40
boundaries of innovation, 135
brain-derived-neurotropic factor (BDNF), 120
brainstorming, 25, 54, 90, 92–96
brainstorming exercises, 96
brainstorming myth, 54
brainstorming session, 95
brainstorming techniques, 108
brainstorming tool, 95
brainteaser, 97
brainwaves, 26

breakthrough ideas, 44, 66, 122–123, 127, 141
breakthrough mojo, 120
breakthrough solutions, 17
breakthrough successes, 49
breakthrough thinking, 119, 125, 128
bureaucracy orientation, 23
bureaucracy processes, 35
business competitiveness, 109
business models, 12, 45, 107, 131, 139
  traditional, 12

C

change management, 62
change management process, 23
change process, 31
change tool, powerful, 99
climate and culture, 89
climate of innovation, 35
climate-creating factors, 60
cognitive complexity/convergent thinking, 84–85
cognitive diversity benefits organisations, 15
cognitive intelligence, 8
cognitive neuroscience research, 65
cognitive psychology, 63
cognitive psychology and neuroscience, 30
cohesive myth, 54
collective CQ, 136
communication and creativity, 144
communication technology, 149
complex intellectual structure, 85
complex social systems, 107
complex solutions, 110
complexity, 3, 43, 60
  idea champions, 23
  increasing, 110
complexity theory, 29
constraints myth, 55
context for creativity, 37, 77
convergent and divergent thinking, 84
convergent response, 84
convergent thinking, 83, 85–87, 108, 111
convergent thinking explained, 84
convergent thinking processes, 86
convergent thinking skills, 86
convergent thinking techniques, 86
CPS, *See* Creative problem solving
CPS techniques, 93
CQ and focus, 39
CQ enhancement training sessions, 89
CQ@Play, 37, 46, 108, 142–143
creative behaviour and innovation, 32
creative characteristics, 109
creative collaboration, 44, 46
creative combinations, 82, 121
creative confidence, 31, 37, 79, 108, 147
creative ideas, 44, 50, 54, 59–60, 69–70, 89, 91, 94
  implementing, 52
creative intelligence, 8–9, 11, 30, 38–39, 41–42, 45–46, 63, 65, 110, 129, 142
  defining, 45
  enhancing, 64

creative leader, 25
creative marketing strategies, 19
creative problem solving (CPS), 58, 77, 88, 90–91, 93
creative thinkers, 89
creative thinking, 10–11, 37, 50, 59, 61–64, 66, 77, 88–89, 91, 93, 99
creative thinking and application of CQ, 61
creative thinking tool, 95
creativity and CQ, 8, 9, 20, 38, 42, 45–46, 65, 91
creativity and creative intelligence, 45
creativity and innovation guidelines, 104
creativity exercises, 80, 101, 104, 147
creativity methodologies, 45, 77, 108
creativity of employees and teams, 50
creativity of individuals and teams, 11
creativity self-test, 51–52
creativity smorgasbord, 144
creativity techniques, 71, 103–104
  advanced, 52
creativity toolkit, 79
creativity tools, 67, 94, 107, 130
  powerful, 57
critical preconditions, establishing, 32
critical thinking, 3, 6, 9–10, 14, 39, 41, 125
critical thinking and creativity, 3
cross-functional process involvement, 34
culture supportive of creativity and innovation, 31–33, 35–36, 44, 66, 104, 147

cyber-chivalry, 3, 20

D

default network (DN), 120, 125
definition of creative intelligence, 45
definition of creativity, 49–51
dependence on convergent thinking, 85
designing games, 107
Design Intelligence and CQ, 41
Design Intelligence and Creative Intelligence, 142
Design Thinking (DT), 3, 41, 43–44, 71, 109–111, 113, 116–117
Design Thinking and innovation, 35
determinants required for creativity and innovation, 33
development of creative intelligence, 45
divergent production abilities, 86
divergent thinking, 79, 84–87, 108
divergent thinking and convergent thinking, 83
divergent thinking exercises, 87
DT, *See* Design Thinking

E

emotional blocks, 55
emotional intelligence, 6, 28, 140
emotions, 6, 40, 42
  positive, 36
empathy map, 111
employee innovativeness, 35

entrepreneurs, 17, 23, 136, 150
examples of CQ, 129
examples of creativity and innovation, 129

F

facial expressions, 130
focus groups, 76
focus mode, 119
focus on creativity, 8
focus on creativity in schools, 8
focused-breakthrough-fear syndrome, 124
Fourth Industrial Revolution, 1–2, 139

G

GNATS, 57–58, 60
goals, 28, 30, 32, 40, 62, 90, 93, 96, 120
  envisaged creative, 75
  innovative, 33
  organisational, 31
  strategic, 9

I

idea-generation phase, 91
ignite breakthroughs, 121, 123
  super tools, 127
ignite creativity and innovation, 33, 109
incentive myth, 54

individual creativity and innovation, 32
individual creativity and innovation shift to team ownership, 32
inert intelligence, measuring, 8
informal creativity networks, 36
innovation, 2–3, 23–24, 26–28, 30–37, 42, 44, 50–51, 70–71, 73, 116–117, 120–121, 129–131, 135–137, 146–147, 149–150
  collaborative, 2
  customer-focused, 30
  empowered, 34
  fundamental, 110
innovation and design thinking, 71
innovation culture, 30, 147
innovation guidelines, 104
innovation intervention, 62
innovative ideas, 37, 54
  excellent, 89
inspiration for ideas, 69
inspiration to action, 80
inspire creativity and innovation, 19
Intellectual Property (IP), 12
intelligences, 6–8, 39–41, 45–46, 59, 63, 84, 86, 108, 142, 146, 150
  distinct, 39
  naturalistic, 40
intelligences and abilities, 6
intervention design, 9, 62
Intranet-based idea bank, 25
Intrapersonal Intelligence, 40
inventions and ideas, 129
inventors, 90, 102, 120, 132
  intrepid, 135

K

key driver of creativity, 33
key underpinning process of
    intelligence, 63
keystone behaviours, 36
killer phrases, 55–57, 66, 103, 114, 123
King Price Insurance, 26
King Price Office Environment
    supporting Creativity, 26
knowledge, 4–6, 12, 14, 16, 23, 33, 44, 49, 64, 75–76, 85, 96, 140–141, 149
  domain, 73
  embodied, 140
  in-depth, 52
  insider, 139, 142
  internalised, 64
knowledge management, 23

L

leadership and empowerment, 23
leadership commitment, 35
leadership model, 28, 30
  emergent, 29
leadership skills, 7
leadership style, 18, 24
  authoritarian, 29
learning, 2, 5–6, 15–16, 20, 44, 48–49, 64, 66, 107, 122, 124, 140, 143, 146, 148
  classroom, 48
  continuous, 81

life-long, 9, 12, 20, 71
learning process, 114
  ever-present, 122
  iterative, 110
learning tool, 107
level of cognitive diversity benefits
    organisations, 15
level of CQ, 22
level of neuroplasticity, 122
Linguistic Intelligence, 39, 41
Little Red Riding Hood, 113
Logical-Mathematical Intelligence, 39
Lone Creator Myth, 54

M

market-making culture, 13
markets, 8, 13, 17, 70, 143
  intended target, 71
  labour, 149
  pop-up, 13
mathematical principles, 130
mental energy and CQ, 142
mental model, 141
  current, 110
mental toughness, 150
metaphorical breakthroughs, 119
mind-maps, 40
  old fashioned, 148
mindset, 6, 44, 80, 91, 126
  agile, 15
  distinct, 29
  organisational, 70
  play-while-you-learn, 8

N

negative definition, 105
neural activity, 123
neural circuit, 122
neural pathways, 65
neural systems, 63
neural zombies, 122
neuroplasticity, 122, 126, 144
neuroscience, 4–5, 30, 63–65, 67
  cognitive, 63, 119
  educational, 5
  social, 29
neuroscience and CQ, 65
neuroscience and creativity, 63
neuro-technological brain enhancements, 139
New World of Work, See NWOW
NWOW (New World of Work), 3, 10, 89

P

problem solving, 14, 41, 44, 53, 77, 92, 124
  complex, 3
  creative, 58, 77, 88, 90, 93
  data-orientated, 42
problem-solving activity, 109
problem-solving capabilities, 2
problem-solving methodologies, 11, 93
problem-solving process, 70
  linear, 110
problem-solving process and creativity, 70
problem-solving sessions, 89
  creative, 89–91, 93
problem-solving teams, 90
  creative, 90
problem-solving techniques, 53, 88
  creative, 90–92
process, creative 3–4, 14, 32, 34–35, 42–43, 47, 49–51, 63–64, 73, 75, 77–78, 89–91, 104, 109–110, 124–128
  breakthrough, 124
  decision-making, 43
  divergent, 86
  intense, 77
  step-by-step, 128
  subconscious, 124
  visualisation, 126
  ideas, 120
  divergent thinking, 86
  information, 69

Q

qualitative information handling techniques, 109
quality of creativity, 54

R

Red Riding Hood (RRH), 113
re-engineer, 35
re-invent, 42, 46, 51, 93, 128
renewed focus on creativity, 8
repetitive learning, 8

responsibility for innovation, 33
retention-boosting techniques, 66
re-tooling ideas, 72
right-brain dominance, 63

S

SCAMPER, 77, 103
SCRAPBOARDS, 103–104
skills, 1, 3, 6–10, 13, 20, 23–24, 41, 44–49, 51, 53, 63, 66, 70, 128, 131
  creative-relevant, 49
  entrepreneurial, 149
  problem-solving, 11, 50, 62, 77, 88
  technical, 7, 14, 33
skills and abilities, 131
skills and creativity, 47
social awareness, 124
social inhibitions, 124
  diminished, 125
social interaction, 140
solitary ideaneers, 95
Spiritual Intelligence, 40, 46
stimulating creativity and innovation, 32, 55

T

target operating model, 44
technological innovation, 134
technology, 1–2, 5, 7, 12–16, 18, 20, 31, 48, 65, 82, 127, 134, 139–140, 143
  brain scan, 64–65
  solar power, 134
technology changes, 10
technology skills, 7
technology-savvy, 16
thinking skills, 49
  divergent, 86
  innovative, 10
thinking styles, 32, 42
thought-paths, 101
tools for understanding and implementing creativity and innovation, 73, 117
triangle test, 88, 108
triarchic theory of intelligence, 41

U

understanding and implementing creativity and innovation, 73
understanding of creativity, 84
understanding of neuroscience, 65
understanding of neuroscience and creative intelligence, 65

W

workforce training programmes, 9
workplace, 7, 14–15, 52, 86
workplace spaces, 10
World Economic Forum, 139
World Intellectual Property Organisation, 136

Y

Youth employment and youth skills
    development initiatives, 12
youth unemployment, 9, 20

www.ingramcontent.com/pod-product-compliance
Lightning Source LLC
Chambersburg PA
CBHW080434230426
43662CB00015B/2271